Making Cordials and Liqueurs at Home

Making Cordials and Liqueurs at Home

❖

JOHN P. FARRELL

HARPER & ROW, PUBLISHERS
New York, Evanston, San Francisco, London

MAKING CORDIALS AND LIQUEURS AT HOME. Copyright © 1974 by John P. Farrell. All rights reserved. Printed in the United States of America. No part of this book may be used or reproduced in any manner whatsoever without written permission except in the case of brief quotations embodied in critical articles and reviews. For information address Harper & Row, Publishers, Inc., 10 East 53rd Street, New York, N.Y. 10022. Published simultaneously in Canada by Fitzhenry & Whiteside Limited, Toronto.

FIRST EDITION

Designed by C. Linda Dingler

Library of Congress Cataloging in Publication Data
Farrell, John Patrick, 1939-
   Making cordials and liqueurs at home.
   Bibliography: p.
   1. Liqueurs. I. Title.
TP611.F37   641.8'72   74-1805
ISBN 0-06-011238-7

To my mother,
who taught me to appreciate books

Contents

Introduction: The Origins of Liqueurs: History and Legends   1

1. Some Basics Concerning Liqueurs   12

2. General Considerations and Directions for Making Your Own Liqueurs   22

    Equipment   22
    Ingredients   24
    Clarifying   32
    Labeling and Keeping a Log   34

3. Recipes for Liqueurs Flavored with Herbs and Spices   36

    Allspice Cordial   40
    Angelica-Based Liqueurs   41
    Anise, Fennel, and Licorice Liqueurs   44
    Drinks Flavored with Caraway Seed: Aquavit, Caraway Cordial, Kümmel, Danzig and Goldwasser   47
    Celery Cordials   50
    Cinnamon and Coriander Cordial   51
    Damiana Liqueur   52
    Ginger Cordials   53
    Juniper Berry Cordial   55
    Lovage Liqueur   55
    Melissa, or Lemon Balm, Liqueur   56
    Mint Liqueurs and Cordials: Crème de Menthe, Peppermint Cordial, Spearmint Cordial   57

  Orris Root Liqueurs 59
  Rosemary Cordials 61
  Tonka Bean Liqueurs 63
  Vanilla Bean Cordial 64
  Verbena, or Lemon Verbena, Cordial 65
  Wormwood Cordial and Absinthe 65
  Zebrovka 69
  Coltea-Blend Herb Liqueur 70

4. Recipes for Fruit-Flavored Cordials and Liqueurs 71

  Apricot Liqueurs 72
  Banana Liqueur 75
  Blackberry Cordial 75
  Currant Cordial or Crème de Cassis 77
  Cherry Liqueurs 78
  Date Cordial 81
  Hawaiian Punch Liqueur 82
  Orange Liqueurs 83
  Other Citrus Fruit Liqueurs: Lemon Cordial, Parfait Amour, Lemon-Lime Liqueur, Grapefruit Liqueurs, Three-Fruit Citrus Liqueur 87
  Peach Liqueur 91
  Pear Cordial 92
  Pineapple Liqueur or Crème de Ananas 93
  Plum Cordial 94
  Prune Cordial 95
  Quince Liqueur 96
  Raspberry Cordial or Crème de Framboises 97
  Maud Grieve's Raspberry Cordial 99
  Strawberry Cordials or Fraises 99
  Rock and Rye 101

5. Miscellaneous Liqueurs and the Use of Extracts 103

  Almond Liqueur 103
  Chocolate Liqueurs or Crème de Cacao 105

Contents

    Coffee Liqueur   107
    Liqueurs Made from Flower Petals: Lavender Liqueur, Orange-Blossom Liqueur, Red-Clover-Blossom Liqueur, Rose-Hip and Anise Liqueur   108
    Tea-Flavored Liqueurs: Black Tea Liqueur, Japanese Green Tea Liqueur   114
    Liqueurs from Extracts   116

Appendix: Tables of Weights, Measures, and Metric Conversions   119

Glossary of Cordials, Liqueurs, and Related Terms   125

Bibliography   137

Index   141

Making Cordials and Liqueurs at Home

Introduction

The Origins of Liqueurs: History and Legend

The history of distilled alcoholic beverages is obscure. Facts are interwoven with folklore, and the entire area is surrounded with fascinating myths and legends. Since liqueurs are a subcategory of distilled beverages, it is worthwhile first to consider the history of alcohol and the development of the art of distillation. Mankind has used alcohol from the very earliest times; very few peoples did not use it in some form or other.

Since natural yeast particles are present in the air, most liquids containing sugar will ferment within a few days after being exposed to it. This explains the amazing diversity of intoxicating drinks. Mead is made from a fermented mixture of honey and water; the juice of grapes, apples, pears, cherries, and other fruit produces wines; grains such as oats, barley, rice, and millet ferment when mixed with water; molasses, palm sap, and even mare's milk in Central Asia are also sources of alcoholic drinks. Before the art of distillation, however, none of these drinks was stronger than beer or wine.

Distillation produces a beverage with a relatively high alcohol content. Alcohol boils at 163° Fahrenheit and water at 212°. Thus if a fermented mixture of low-alcohol content is heated above 163° but below 212° the alcohol is boiled off. A still is an apparatus which collects and cools these vapors to yield a liquid with a high alcohol content. Strong alcohols can also be produced by cooling, since water freezes at 32° Fahrenheit and alcohol freezes at −237°. The process here would involve cooling a weak alcohol mixture and straining out the ice crystals. Curiously, the cooling process is very rare. The only instance that I have found of its use to produce beverages is a rather crude drink made by farmers in a rural part of New Jersey, and they call it Jersey Lightning; in extreme cold spells barrels of fermented apple cider are placed outside the barn, and when the cider is partially frozen, the ice is removed.

The method of distillation by heat evolved and spread slowly. There are references to the process as early as 800 B.C. in China and India, but the use of the process was not widespread. There are references to some crude forms of distillation in Roman writings. For example, there is mention of sailors boiling sea water and catching the vapors in sponges to obtain drinkable water, and Pliny, who wrote at approximately A.D. 30, relates that turpentine was obtained by boiling pine pitch and gathering the

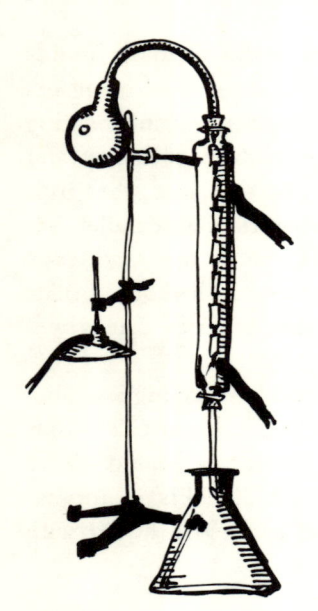

Distillation process

Introduction: The Origins of Liqueurs

vapors in wool. Apparently the possibility that the same might be done with wine did not occur to the Romans. Considering their excesses with wine, however, this may have been fortunate for their civilization. Drinks made by mixing herbs in sweetened wine were used for medicinal purposes by both the Greeks and the Romans, and these beverages were probably very similar to some modern liqueurs except for the low alcohol content. Many medicinal herbs of that period are now used as flavorings.

It was not until the Middle Ages that the distillation of alcohol became widespread in Europe. Medieval alchemists employed the process throughout Europe in an attempt to achieve their two goals, turning base metals into gold and developing an elixir to prolong life. As H. J. Grossman, in his *Guide to Wines, Spirits, and Beers*, says: "If the medieval magician did not learn how to prolong life at least he learned the secret of making it more interesting, for it was his experiments which produced the first cordials." Other liqueurs were also developed during this time by individuals who tried to produce love potions, aphrodisiacs, and cures for various ailments. By the time of the Renaissance, it had become quite fashionable among European nobility to employ liqueurmakers who concentrated on flavor. Their products came to be served on the occasions that treaties and pacts were ratified and thus became known as ratafias.

The origin of many liqueurs is surrounded by legends, a few of which are recounted here. It must be remembered that in times prior to the advent of large national taxes on distilled alcohol it was possible to do considerably more experimentation with a far smaller financial investment. In most countries today at least 80 percent of the retail cost of alcoholic beverages goes for taxes.

One illustration of the lower cost of distilled spirits in previous times is provided by an incident related in *Larousse Gastronomique*, which describes a party given in 1552 by Sir Edward Kennel, commander of the English navy. He had a huge bowl constructed into which was poured 80 barrels of brandy, more than 1,000 pounds of sugar, plus a large amount of citrus fruit and Malaga wine. The guests were served by a ship's boy who floated on this artificial lake in a rosewood boat. No boy could perform this task for more than a quarter of an hour before he became intoxicated from the vapors given off by this enormous amount of alcohol, and the server had to be replaced at regular intervals. This incident explains some of the older European liqueur recipes in which the finished liqueur may equal a barrel or more.

An example of a modern liqueur with a very old recipe and a past surrounded by legend is Strega, a delicious liqueur flavored with angelica and a number of other herbs with a secret formula. Many connoisseurs consider this to be the best liqueur made in Italy. A recipe providing a fairly close simulation is given on page 44. According to legend this liqueur was developed as a love potion by three beautiful witches in the city of Benevento. The legend states that the drink has magical properties, and if two lovers share it they will never part.

Absinthe is probably surrounded by more apocryphal myths and stories than any other liqueur. Various recipes are given on pages 67 and 68. It is a liqueur based on wormwood or *Artemisia absinthium*, one of the most bitter herbs in existence. Commercial varieties were generally made with wormwood collected in the Jura Mountains of Switzerland, where the essential oils in the plant were of a particularly high concentration. The liqueur was generally flavored with other herbs, especially anise, to partially mask the wormwood, and the alcohol content was generally quite high, often 136 proof. Various mind-altering and aphrodisiacal properties were attributed to the drink, and stories about it caught the imaginations of many people. Expensive Parisian brothels capitalized on these stories by serving guests a cup of coffee, a croissant, and a glass of absinthe. Feelings of mental alertness and well-being are also attributed to absinthe. As explained in Chapter 3, wormwood does have slight stimulant properties and some medicinal benefits, but the properties attributed

Introduction: The Origins of Liqueurs

to it by legend are exaggerated. Large amounts of wormwood are toxic, but stories of its precipitating violence should not be taken too seriously. Following a celebrated case in which an absinthe drinker killed his wife and child and then attempted suicide, Switzerland prohibited the manufacture of absinthe in 1908. The individual involved, however, had severe psychological problems previously and was an alcoholic. Nevertheless the public clamor named absinthe as the culprit. As the prohibition movement gathered force, other countries also banned absinthe. After France prohibited it, the Pernod Fils Company manufactured it in Spain until the Spanish Civil War. It was during the period between the two world wars that American expatriate writers living in Europe, notably Ernest Hemingway, became acquainted with the absinthe made in Spain and helped perpetuate the myths surrounding it. Absinthe is now banned throughout most of the world, and the absinthe substitutes on the market contain no wormwood. Very small amounts of wormwood are permitted in the manufacture of vermouth, and some people believe this gives martinis an aphrodisiac effect beyond the relaxation effects of the alcohol itself. However, there is no solid evidence for any sexual effects whatever from wormwood, and if it does have any minor mind-altering effects, these are not very dramatic. In view of its rather bitter taste, I cannot understand why any person seeking psychedelic thrills would even try it.

A liqueur with an interesting past is Benedictine. It is believed to have been developed by a Benedictine monk, Dom Bernardo Vincelli, in 1510. He was seeking an elixir to treat the fevers from malaria which were a problem for both the monks and the peasant farmers and fishermen in the vicinity of the abbey at Fécamp. The fame of the liqueur quickly spread, and in 1534 it was sampled and praised by Francis I, who was then king of France. The abbey was destroyed during the French Revolution, but the recipe was saved. Although it has not been made by monks since that time, every bottle still bears the letters D.O.M., an abbreviation for *Deo Optimo Maximo*, which means: "To

God, most good, most great." The recipe for this liqueur is a closely guarded secret. It is made with a number of herbs, and it is said that many of the flavors are distilled out separately and then blended together. Only three people know the complete details of the process. Many people have tried to duplicate the flavor, myself included, but no one has quite been able to do it. At the distillery in Fécamp there is a collection of hundreds of examples of commercial attempts to duplicate it. Apparently the belief persists that this unique and delicious liqueur has medicinal benefits. Peter Hallgarten, in his book *Liqueurs*, reports that large quantities of it are used by the tin miners of Malaysia, who have a particular problem with pains in their joints and muscles because the mines are often knee deep in water.

Another French liqueur with an interesting background is Chartreuse. There are two varieties of Chartreuse, a yellow and a green. A simulation of the yellow is possible with the recipe on page 42. A white Chartreuse was also made at one time, but it is no longer manufactured. These liqueurs are actually made by Carthusian monks at their abbey near Grenoble in the French Alps. Although the order was founded at that location in 1084, the liqueur formulas were not developed until later. The basis for the secret formulas was given to the monks by the Marechal d'Estrées in 1607, and they were further developed and perfected by Brother Manbec, an apothecary at the monastery, in the 1750s. The liqueurs were used mainly by the monks for medicinal purposes. They were not manufactured on a large scale until the mid-1800s. In 1848 some army officers were quartered at the monastery, and they were served one of the liqueurs after dinner. They were amazed at the delicious flavor and spread its reputation widely. By 1860 a large distillery had to be built to accommodate demand. Unfortunately for the monks, their order was expelled from France shortly after the turn of the century. During this period of exile from France the monks began making their liqueur at Tarragona in Spain. Connoisseurs debated as to

Introduction: The Origins of Liqueurs

whether there were detectable differences between Chartreuse made at Tarragona and that made at the original location, but all agreed that a commercial attempt to replicate the beverage in France with some government involvement was a poor imitation. By 1931 the French government was obliged by litigation to restore the property of the Carthusian monks. The formulas are still secret, and the process for the green variety is said to involve as many as five separate distillations. I may be mistaken, but my taste buds and nose tell me that the green variety contains a hint of wormwood.

Shifting attention from France to the British Isles, there is an interesting legend concerning the Scotch liqueur Drambuie. This title means "the drink that satisfies" in Gaelic. According to legend, the recipe for this liqueur was originally a secret formula which belonged to Prince Charles Edward Stuart or Bonnie Prince Charlie. Like other nobles of his day, the young pretender to the British throne had favorite liqueurs that were made according to secret recipes by trusted members of his staff, and these beverages were served on occasions of state. In 1745 the prince returned from France and raised an army of Scottish Highlanders in rebellion. This army was disastrously defeated the following year at the Battle of Culloden Moor. A large price was offered for the capture of the prince, and he was hunted through the western part of Scotland. He was sheltered by the MacKinnon family on the Isle of Skye, and they eventually brought him to the Scottish mainland, from which a ship took him safely to France. The Prince is reputed to have given MacKinnon the secret recipe for his favorite liqueur as an expression of gratitude. The MacKinnon family, however, did not market the liqueur commercially until 1892.

There is a controversy about the origin of a liqueur similar to Drambuie, Irish Mist. Irish Mist has a base of Irish whiskey rather than Scotch, and therefore it does not have the slight smoky flavor that is present in Drambuie. Irish Mist is also somewhat drier, but it has a similar extraordinary smoothness that stems from the use of heather honey as the sweetener in both liqueurs. The controversy around this delicious Irish liqueur centers on when and where it was first made. Hallgarten, in his *Liqueurs*, states that it began shortly after the Second World War when the production of Glen Mist was moved from Scotland to Ireland. Because of the austerity in England in 1945, supplies of honey and Scotch whiskey were unavailable, so production of Glen Mist was transferred to Tullamore in Ireland until 1963. During this period commercial production of Irish Mist began as a joint venture of Irish interests by Severmo Ltd. and S. F. Hallgarten of Glen Mist. Most other authorities on liqueurs believe that it is far older. H. J. Grossman, in his authoritative *Guide to Wines, Spirits, and Beers*, indicates that it has very old origins, but that the recipe was lost for two centuries. I believe that Grossman is correct because the tradition of flavoring whiskey with herbs and sweetening it with the remarkably smooth heather honey produced there is very ancient in Ireland and it goes back almost to the time that whiskey was introduced in that country, approximately A.D. 1100.

Another liqueur made in the British Isles that is of interest because of its ancient use is sloe gin. It is really a liqueur rather than a gin, and it is flavored with the wild sloe berry. This berry is the fruit of the blackthorn bush, a relative of the plum, and the wood of this bush is remarkably hard, durable, and flexible. This wood is the source of the shillelagh, a weapon originating in prehistoric times, which is remarkably effective for subduing an attacking man or beast.

Sloe gin is highly esteemed in Britain as a remedy for digestive complaints. The Pedlar brand, made by the Hawker firm of Plymouth, has been sold to the Royal Household for more than three hundred years. Each year when the sloe berries ripen a large group of women from Plymouth pick the wild sloes of Cornwall and Devon for this firm. As with the fine *eaux de vie*

Introduction: The Origins of Liqueurs

made on the European continent, only perfectly unblemished fruit is used.

In northern Europe there is an interesting legend concerning kümmel, a liqueur flavored with caraway seed. Caraway seed are often used to impart flavor to rye bread and cheese, and they are an excellent aid to digestion. Holland is one of the largest producers of caraway seeds; they have been cultivated there at least since the Middle Ages. In Amsterdam in 1575 Lucas Bols began making the earliest kümmel of which a record can be found. Peter the Great of Russia visited Holland on a trip to Europe in the late 1690s to learn European industrial techniques so that he might modernize Russia. He was particularly interested in learning shipbuilding techniques to establish an effective Russian navy. Therefore he hid his identity and labored as a carpenter in an Amsterdam shipyard. This genius of a man, who was, however, also tinged with madness and sadism, had the constitution of a bear and occasionally took part in stupendous orgies and drinking bouts. Kümmel was one form of alcohol that he became especially fond of during this stay in Amsterdam, and his lodgings were not far from the Bols distillery. He is reputed to have brought kümmel with him on his return, and this is supposedly the source of kümmel production in Russia and Latvia. Some believe that kümmel production did not begin until a later date in that area, but nevertheless, for many years a variety of kümmels of very high quality were produced in Latvia. Some of the famous distilleries there included that of the Wolfschmidt family in the city of Riga, one on the estate of Allash, and one on the estate of Count Pahlen. Unfortunately the Mentzendorff family which made the original Allash kümmel fled after the First World War, and other families in the production had to flee in the Nazi era. This, plus the destruction brought about by the war, ended the kümmel industry in Latvia. Although individuals from the families involved have resumed production of their respective kümmels in other countries, connoisseurs feel that they are not quite of their original quality, and judge Gilka kümmel, made in Germany, to be the finest of the ones currently produced.

The use of gold flecks in liqueurs became quite widespread in the Middle Ages, and a liqueur related to kümmel, Goldwasser, survives as an example of this as related in the discussion of the recipe on page 50. The origin of this practice stems from the old European belief that gold is a cure-all. In the *Canterbury Tales*, Geoffrey Chaucer says, "Gold in phisik is a cordial."

An apocryphal story surrounds the origin of liqueurs flavored with flower petals. Supposedly in fifteenth-century Padua a physician was pestered by a hypochondriacal but rich and powerful woman. He cleverly thought of treating her with a pleasant-tasting but harmless placebo and mixed together brandy, honey, and perfume extracted from roses. Some claim this is the origin of the rosolios, or flower-petal liqueurs. At any rate the popularity of these drinks quickly spread, and it is historically known that when Catherine de' Medici left Florence to marry the Duc d'Orléans, who later became Henry II of France, there were several individuals who were skilled in making this type of liqueur among the staff that accompanied her. Rose-petal-flavored liqueurs are still popular in Italy and the eastern Mediterranean area.

There is an interesting story concerning Calvados (which, strictly speaking, is not a liqueur, since it is unsweetened, but an apple brandy or apple *eau de vie*). Approximately a thousand years ago Vikings captured Normandy, and it was formally ceded to them by Charles III, called Charles the Simple, of France in 911. The Vikings in this group settled there and accepted the French language and Christianity but retained many of their Norse customs, especially a lusty approach to eating and drinking. Normandy was rich in apple orchards, and distilled apple brandy was soon developed. During the eleventh century it was found that a glass of apple brandy taken straight in one or two gulps in the middle of a meal increases the appetite and allows

Introduction: The Origins of Liqueurs

one to consume more food. This customary drink in the middle of the meal persists to the present day and is called "Trou Normand," which literally means "Norman hole," since the purpose of it is to make a hole or space for more food. When served at the conclusion of a meal, Calvados is sipped rather than gulped. Although true Calvados imported from France is rather expensive, some of the applejack brandies made in the United States, for example the Laird brand, come close to it in flavor and smoothness at considerably less cost.

These are just a few of the fascinating legends that surround the various liqueurs. If you wish to pursue them further, other sources are listed in the bibliography.

1

Some Basics Concerning Liqueurs

More and more people are coming to enjoy cordials and liqueurs, especially when they are served with coffee after a good meal. Figures from the Distilled Spirits Institute, which collects and prepares statistical information for the alcohol beverage industry in the United States, show that the sale of liqueurs more than doubled in ten years, from 12 million gallons in 1963 to more than 26 million gallons in 1972. Most of the supply was produced in the United States, with about 12 percent being imported. (The bulk of the imported liqueurs comes from Italy, France, the United Kingdom, and Mexico in that order.)

Obviously a book like this must raise the question: Is it really worthwhile to make your own? It is, from a number of standpoints, but economy should be considered first. Most of the better liqueurs cost more than $8 per bottle, and if you check the label closely, you will find that most liqueur bottles hold only 23 ounces. An example of the savings from making your own can be seen from the recipe in this book for a coffee liqueur very close to Kahlúa in flavor that comes out to a cost of $2.50 for 23 ounces. Even for liqueurs that are relatively expensive to simulate, there are still considerable savings. Drambuie, with Scotch whisky as an alcohol base, costs approximately 22 cents per ounce to make, while Drambuie costs approximately 39 cents

Some Basics Concerning Liqueurs

per ounce when a bottle is purchased in a liquor store. Thus the savings is close to 50 percent. Most of the time it is greater than that. O Cha, a delicious Japanese liqueur based on green tea, costs $8.50 for a 19-ounce bottle, or approximately 44 cents per ounce. A very similar liqueur can be prepared in your own kitchen, with commercial vodka as a base, at a cost of about 12 cents per ounce. Hence your savings would be close to 350 percent.

In addition to economy, there are other reasons for making your own liqueurs. Like the large food producers, commercial makers of alcoholic beverages have been questioned in regard to the purity and wholesomeness of their products. When you make your own liqueurs, you can be certain that there are no harmful chemical additives for color or flavor.

Another, and perhaps the best, reason for making your own liqueurs is that you can adjust the results to your own personal taste. Like many people, I find commercial crème-type liqueurs and cordials far too sweet for my taste; yet if you dilute these to make them less sweet the flavor is also weakened. In making my own, I simply use less sweetening. How sweet or dry the liqueur is can be precisely controlled when you make your own, and this is only one of the many characteristics you can adjust. Other advantages you can give your homemade liqueur are the extra smoothness and flavor that can be obtained by using honey rather than sugar as a sweetener and the endless varieties of flavors that come from various combinations and permutations of spices, herbs, and other flavorings.

A few words are necessary about definitions. Although at one time a distinction was made, liqueur and cordial have become synonymous terms. U.S. Treasury regulations require that products marketed under these terms be at least 2½ percent sugar by weight, although most commercial products are a good deal higher than that. Their alcohol content varies widely: For some it is in the vicinity of 40 proof and not much stronger than fortified wines, and for others, such as green Chartreuse, it exceeds 100 proof. Most, however, are between 60 and 70 proof. Liqueurs can be flavored with herbs, spices, fruit, coffee, tea, chocolate, nuts, flower petals, and other ingredients. Sometimes the ingredients are not even of plant origin; substances such as amber and musk have been included in liqueurs.

One source of confusion in definitions concerning liqueurs and cordials is that brandies flavored with fruit and sweetened with sugar are liqueurs, while fruit brandies distilled from fermented fruits are not liqueurs, yet both are called fruit brandy. Examples of the former are blackberry-, cherry-, and apricot-flavored brandies, which are actually grape brandy flavored with these fruits and sweetened with sugar. These are considered cordials or liqueurs, and should not be confused with true fruit brandies, which in Europe are called *eaux de vie*. *Eaux de vie* are unsweetened, clear white, and distilled from particular fermented fruits. Examples are kirsch, which is made from cherries; framboise from raspberries; and mirabelle from plums. The best *eaux de vie* are made in Switzerland and very expensive; $12 to $15 per fifth is not unusual. Their cost is high because the Swiss use only perfect hand-picked fruit. If a fruit has a blemish, it is not used. Swiss-produced *eau de vie* often has a fruit in the bottle: for example, a Williams pear in the bottom of a bottle of poire-William. I often wondered how they got such a large fruit into a bottle with a small opening; I am told that it is done by putting the bottle over the pear when it starts growing on the tree.

Ratafia is another term used in connection with liqueurs and cordials. In some places ratafia is simply another synonym for liqueur; in others it refers to liqueurs made by steeping or infusing flavoring in an alcohol base. This is the way all homemade liqueurs are prepared. Many commercial liqueurs are also produced this way, but most producers distill the alcohol base after the flavoring has steeped and then add sweetening and coloring. As noted in the Introduction, the term "ratafia" comes from the

Some Basics Concerning Liqueurs

Renaissance era, when these beverages were invariably served on the occasion of signing an agreement or treaty between monarchs. In those days liqueurmaking, or cordialmaking, was a highly respected art, and such figures as Louis XIV and Catherine de' Medici considered their liqueurmakers among the most valuable artisans in their employ.

There are other definitions related to liqueurs that are somewhat less general. In French nomenclature the word "double" or "triple" in the label refers to the strength of the flavor. A liqueur with the word "double" would have a strong and pronounced flavor, and one with "triple" even more so; for example, the Grand Marnier label states "triple orange" to indicate that it is a full-flavored drink. Terms with the root word "fine" on French labels refer to the strength of the alcohol content. Demi-fines have a low, fines a moderate, and surfines a high alcohol content. Crème indicates that the liqueur has a high sugar content, which makes it sweet and gives it a creamlike consistency. Huiles or baums are also sweet. The terms *eau, eaux,* and *extraits* indicate that there is a low sugar content, if the liqueur is sweetened at all, and that the consistency is thin, like water rather than cream.

In German nomenclature relating to liqueurs and similar beverages the word *Wasser* indicates that the product was distilled from fermented fruit; for example, Kirschwasser is distilled from fermented cherries. The word *Geist* indicates that the sugar content of the original fruit may have been too low for fermentation and that the fruit was infused in alcohol; this mixture may have been distilled or filtered. The German word *Geist* means spirit. Another German term that appears occasionally is *Branntwein* (literally "burned wine"); this term refers to a distilled brandy or *eau de vie*. *Eis Liköre* on German labels indicates a liqueur intended to be served over ice. *Kristal Liköre* indicates that the liqueur is very sweet and that some of the sugar content has crystallized out.

At this point it is appropriate to explain something of how

liqueurs and cordials are manufactured commercially. There are three basic methods: infusion, percolation, and distillation. The process of infusion, sometimes called maceration, is much like brewing tea. Herbs or fruits are infused, or steeped, in alcohol until their flavor thoroughly permeates the liquid. This is the method used for home production of liqueurs, and it is used industrially to obtain delicate flavors that would be broken down by heat. In percolation the process employed in percolating coffee is used, although in a closed system, so that the alcohol does not boil away. When this process is used industrially, the percolation for liqueurs may continue for weeks rather than minutes. Distillation is probably the most common industrial technique in liqueur production. Most commercial liqueurs are produced by distilling an infusion of alcohol and flavoring ingredients such as herbs or fruit. Distillation is based on the principle that alcohol boils at a lower temperature than water, so by heating a water-alcohol mixture to a point below the boiling point of water but higher than that of alcohol, the alcohol can be boiled off. An apparatus is necessary to collect these alcohol vapors and cool them so that they return to the liquid state. At various times and in different cultures many ingenious stills have been devised. It is reputed that some of the very distinctive liqueurs such as Char-

Types of glasses for serving liqueurs

Some Basics Concerning Liqueurs

treuse which are made by secret processes are distilled as many as five times.

When fruits are involved, they are usually fermented and then distilled and sweetened. However, when herbs or fruits that are difficult to ferment are used, they may be infused first and then the infusion distilled.

A great deal has been written about the proper way to serve liqueurs. Much of it is nonsense, especially when it comes to glassware. For strongly aromatic liqueurs, a simple pony glass with straight sides is all that is necessary. When one is serving a liqueur with a milder and more delicate aroma, a brandy snifter which funnels the aroma toward the nostrils is best.

It is interesting to explore the effect of temperature on liqueurs. Some—for example, caraway- or anise-flavored ones—are good icy cold. If you do not want to dilute them with ice you can chill both the bottle and the glasses in the freezer. Stemmed glasses are good for such liqueurs because the hand will not raise the temperature of the drink and they are also more comfortable to hold. Other liqueurs, especially herb-flavored ones with a delicate aroma and a brandy base, are very good when warmed slightly. The brandy warmers sold in specialty shops will do for this, or you can simply pour the amount you wish to serve at a given time into a Pyrex measuring cup and set it for a few minutes in a pan of hot water. Liqueurs may also be served with ice, either "on the rocks" or over shaved or crushed ice (this drink is called a frappé). One of my favorites is the simulation of Drambuie (see p. 43) over crushed ice.

In France many cordials are served in a glass of mineral water; crème de menthe, for example, is almost invariably served this way. A good drink and a remarkably effective remedy for mild nausea or indigestion from overeating is one ounce of crème de menthe with ice in a tall glass of soda water.

Liqueurs and cordials can be used in mixed drinks both for the flavor and for the smoothness they impart to a drink. One

Various ways of serving liqueurs

Parfaits made with liqueurs and cordials

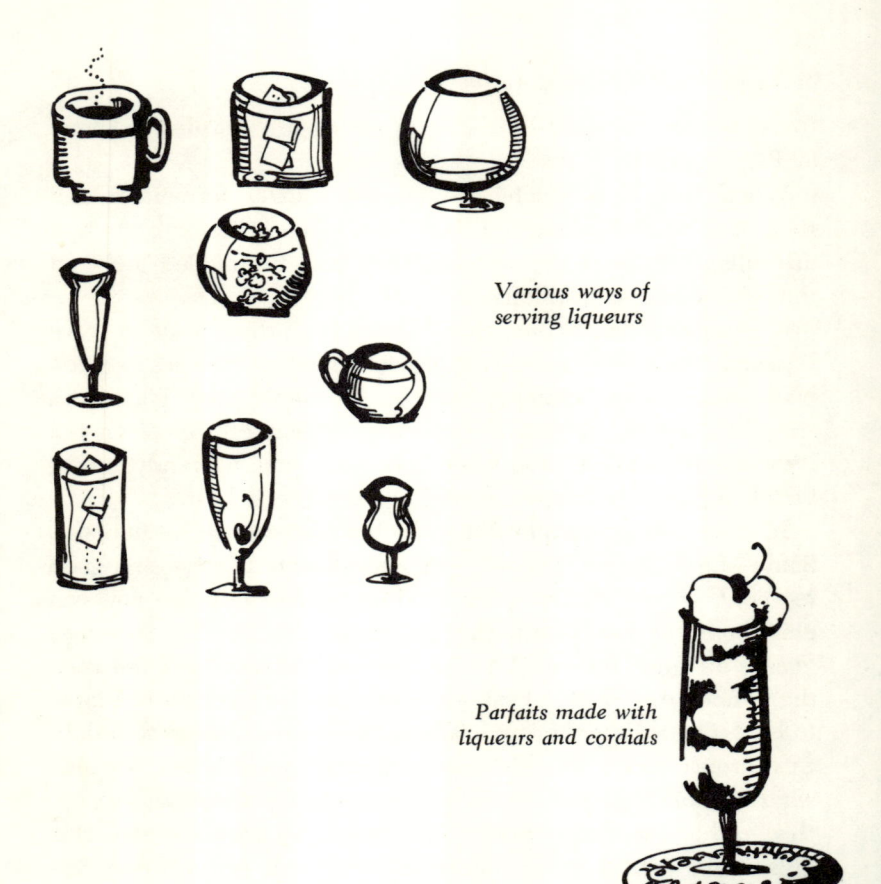

Flambéing with liqueurs and cordials

Some Basics Concerning *Liqueurs*

mixed drink containing several liqueurs is the pousse-café, which consists of layers of various liqueurs in the same glass. An example would be to have Benedictine, orange liqueur, and cherry liqueur all in the same glass but in layers rather than mixed. This is rather difficult to make, but the trick is to pour each successive layer slowly over the back of a spoon. It also helps if you know the specific gravity, which is the weight per given volume, of each liqueur. The liqueurs should be poured with the heaviest first and progressively going to lighter ones. It is difficult to determine the specific gravity of homemade liqueurs, but there is a good table for commercial liqueurs in *Grossman's Guide to Wines, Spirits, and Beers*, which is listed in the bibliography.

Liqueurs can also be used in the preparation of food, especially desserts. They make very good toppings on ice cream, puddings, and fruit. Numerous liqueurs go well on vanilla ice cream or pudding. Some that you may want to try first are cherry, coffee, chocolate, and crème de menthe. Tall parfait glasses permit you to vary the flavors of ice cream for more interesting combinations.

An elegant and easy-to-prepare dessert is to alternate layers of liqueur and ice cream in parfait glasses. You can have a single liqueur and a single ice-cream flavor, or you can use two varieties of either one or two varieties of both. For the single type, good combinations are mint liqueur on either vanilla or chocolate or chocolate liqueur on coffee ice cream. Many fruit liqueurs such as cherry are also good on vanilla. A pleasant combination of two varieties is to start with mint liqueur, add some vanilla ice cream, add some chocolate liqueur, then more ice cream, and so on. Since most liqueurs go well with ice cream, do not be afraid to experiment, but it is a good idea to test the concoction first with a few drops of liqueur and a teaspoon of ice cream. Top parfaits with whipped cream and either a cherry or shredded chocolate.

Many liqueurs are also good on fruit. Some interesting combinations are mint on pineapple or grapefruit; orange liqueurs on citrus fruits, berries, apricots, or peaches; blackberry on grapefruit, peaches, or pears; and cherry on cherries or pineapple. A delicious dessert can be made by marinating the fruit in the liqueur and then using this as a topping.

For something spectacular you can flambé a combination of fruit and ice cream. Cherries jubilee is a good example of such a flambéed dessert. The cherries are marinated in cherry liqueur, served over vanilla ice cream, and topped with flaming brandy. Commercial producers of alcoholic beverages market high-proof rums and other products especially intended for flambéing, but these are completely unnecessary. You can flambé with liqueurs above 70 proof with little difficulty if you know the secret of warming the liqueur and the utensil it is served from. One good way is to put three ounces of liqueur in a Pyrex measuring cup and set it in a small saucepan of boiling water until the liqueur warms. It also helps to warm the ladle that is used to pour the flaming liqueur over the food. This can be done by immersing it in boiling water. Ignite the liqueur in the ladle or other container before it is poured.

There are also many ways to use liqueurs in nondessert cooking, but to treat this topic adequately would require almost a book of its own. The most common way is probably as an addition to gravy or to the liquid used to baste roast meats. Good combinations here are: peach, apricot, or cherry liqueurs on baked ham; orange liqueur on chicken or duck; and kümmel on roast pork.

In concluding this chapter on basics about liqueurs, I wish to make a few comments regarding the source of these recipes and how I got started making my own. Many years ago when I was a typically impoverished graduate student, I enjoyed liqueurs but could seldom afford them. During this period a friend who was a recent graduate of pharmacy school was drafted into the army and stationed in a large army pharmaceutical laboratory. Since he had some free time and a lot of precise measuring equipment

Some Basics Concerning Liqueurs

available, he attempted to develop a recipe which duplicated some of the better coffee liqueurs on the market and eventually came up with the recipe for coffee liqueur which with some minor alteration is presented in this book. This started me on the road to developing recipes to duplicate other liqueurs, and I was also given some recipes by friends, usually on an exchange basis.

A number of sources, especially French and German ones, were consulted in the development of these recipes, but such sources were used only as starting points. In every case recipes were considerably modified: (1) to adapt them to an American audience and system of measurement; (2) to reduce them to workable quantities for the average household (most European recipes in this area are intended for innkeepers or bartenders and therefore call for huge quantities such as a barrel of brandy); and (3) to simplify the procedure for making them without a sacrifice in flavor. An example of this last item is to shorten steeping time by using either larger quantities of flavoring ingredients or a different part of a plant; leaves, for example, have a shorter steeping time than seeds or roots. These recipes are presented after considerable experimentation, and all of them have been fully tested. I hope that they are used by those who wish to explore the myriad of pleasurable flavors and aromas that can be obtained from the many herbs, fruits, and other botanicals available; and I hope too that the results of the recipes are used in moderation.

2

General Considerations and Directions for Making Your Own Liqueurs

EQUIPMENT

Little in the way of tools and equipment is required in liqueur-making, and the few items that are needed are simple and inexpensive. A funnel, a measuring cup, a strainer, and some clean white cotton cloth for filtering are all that are really necessary. Other items that are useful although not really required include a mortar and pestle for crushing herbs and spices, a balance or dietary scale, a funnel holder, and laboratory glassware, especially Erlenmeyer flasks. These flasks are especially useful because they have a wide base and low center of gravity and therefore they almost never tip or get knocked over. This is something that I appreciate when I am making a liqueur with an expensive alcohol base such as Scotch whiskey.

Filter paper, which gives finer filtering than cloth, can be obtained in most hobby shops and chemical-supply houses. I don't use it because I find I can get just as effective filtering with two or three layers of cloth. If you want to use it, get the fastest or most porous available. Three or four feet of plastic tubing, which is useful for siphoning, can be purchased at hobby shops or pet shops that carry tropical fish or aquarium supplies.

Equipment for home liqueurmaking

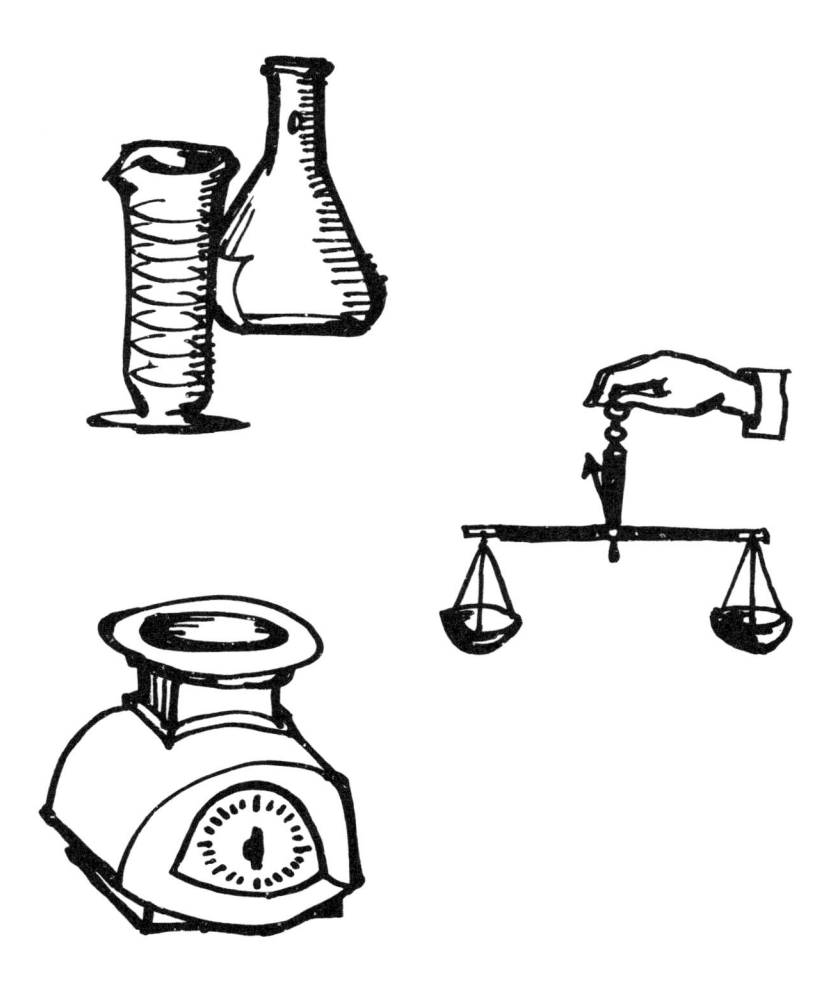

Most European recipes are in the metric system, and they also frequently specify amounts of ingredients by weight. The table of equivalents on page 122 should be of value in handling this.

Obviously, you will need bottles for your finished product. Used wine and liqueur bottles or decanters are best for this, especially when serving liqueurs to guests. It is amazing how much an attractive bottle influences people's perception of a homemade liqueur. I have heard otherwise intelligent people say that a homemade liqueur was just OK when served out of a used fruit jar with a pasted label showing the ingredients, and on another occasion say that same liqueur was fantastically good when served out of a fancy bottle. It is essential to emphasize that plastic containers should never be used in storing or making liqueurs. I have had the experience of having liqueurs ruined from steeping in a glass jar with an unlined plastic cap. A plastic taste and odor permeates the entire contents within a week.

INGREDIENTS

The necessary ingredients for homemade liqueurs include: the alcohol base; sweetening; water; coloring; and a source of flavoring, which may be herbs, spices, fruits, flower petals, or a prepared extract. Glycerine may be added to give body. Each of these will be considered in turn.

Alcohol Base

Obviously, only commercially prepared alcohol on which the taxes have already been paid should be used as the base. In addition to the legal risks involved, distilling your own or using laboratory ethyl alcohol can be dangerous. Stills for alcohol have a tendency to blow up. Also, many cheap stills are handmade of copper with the seams soldered with lead. As a result lead compounds work their way into the alcohol, and many a moonshiner has a damaged nervous system from lead poisoning.

General Considerations and Directions 25

Ordinary commercial vodka is the most useful base. I recommend a vodka which states on the label that it has been charcoal-filtered, because this process removes any slight impurities which may affect the flavor of your material. Since there is little difference in the character or flavor of charcoal-filtered vodkas, the cheapest of those available will suffice. Generally, 80-proof vodka is the most useful, especially if your recipe calls for steeping a flavoring such as herbs or spices and then filtering. For a stronger drink, however, you may want to use 90-proof vodka. Usually if you are going to add one cup of sugar syrup for sweetening, 80-proof vodka is sufficient. If two cups of sweetening are used, 90- or 100-proof vodka may be preferable. 100-proof vodka is also best with presweetened commercial extracts for liqueurs such as those prepared by Spice Club, Inc. The proofs of finished liqueurs, depending on the amount of sweetening and the starting proof of the alcohol base, are given in Tables 1 and 2.

TABLE 1

Final Proof of Finished Liqueur Using 24 Ounces Alcohol Base and 8 Ounces Sweetening Syrup

STRENGTH OF ALCOHOL BASE	FINAL PROOF OF LIQUEUR
80 proof vodka or brandy	60 proof
86 proof whiskey	64.5 proof
90 proof vodka	67.5 proof
100 proof vodka	75 proof

TABLE 2

Final Proof of Finished Liqueur Using 24 Ounces Alcohol Base and 16 Ounces Sweetening Syrup

STRENGTH OF ALCOHOL BASE	FINAL PROOF OF LIQUEUR
80 proof vodka or brandy	48 proof
86 proof whiskey	51.6 proof
90 proof vodka	54 proof
100 proof vodka	60 proof

Note that in the United States proof is defined as twice the percent of alcohol content. To convert proof to percent of alcohol content, simply halve the proof number.

Since proof means exactly twice the percent alcohol in the beverage, an 80-proof beverage would have 40 percent alcohol. In England and France proof is defined differently, and the values of the tables would not hold for products from these countries. In the British system 100 percent alcohol equals 175 proof, whereas in the United States it would equal 200 proof. This curious British system is called the Sykes system after the man who developed it. Hundred-proof Sykes would equal approximately 110 proof in the United States. Sykes based his system on the fact that if alcohol of 100° Sykes is mixed with gunpowder, the mixture will burn. If the alcohol strength is lower, the mixture will not ignite and it is called "under proof." Mixtures of strong concentrations of alcohol are called "over proof" if they produce an explosive result in combination with gunpowder. I have not yet been able to find out if Mr. Sykes survived to a ripe old age. The French define alcohol content in Gay-Lussac units, or GL. Their system is the most rational because the GL is equal to the percent of alcohol by volume, and a beverage that is 40 percent alcohol would be 40° GL.

In addition to vodka, other sources of alcohol for liqueurmaking include brandy, rum, gin, whiskey, and grain neutral spirits. Grain neutral spirits are usually available in the larger liquor stores at approximately 190 proof. This is excellent for making liqueurs based on citrus fruits (using recipes in the fruit section of this book), because the aromatic oils from the fruit rind are absorbed very efficiently at high concentrations of alcohol. Obviously, the mixture must be diluted with water before consuming.

Brandy is a good alcohol base for liqueurs because it has a pleasing flavor of its own that blends well with most fruit and herb flavorings. Since the flavoring of your liqueur will mask subtle qualities of the brandy, it is totally unnecessary to use fine imported cognacs. The less expensive domestic brands, such as Masson, Almadén, Christian Brothers, or Coronet, make a fine base for liqueurs. Sometimes when I am making a liqueur with a delicate flavor and I want some, but not too much, brandy flavor in the finished product, I use a base of half brandy and half vodka.

Rum, at least to my taste, goes well with fruit flavors, especially citrus and berries, and also coffee flavoring. Gin has a rather distinctive taste, and I find that it goes well with sloe berries or mint but with little else. Whiskey is also somewhat limited because of its strong characteristic flavor, but it is good for some cordials such as "rock and rye" and liqueurs sweetened with honey and flavored with herbs. Commercial examples are Irish Mist and Drambuie, which have Irish whisky and Scotch bases respectively.

The cheapest way to get alcohol for liqueurmaking is to buy vodka by the half-gallon. Most of the recipes in this book call for a fifth of alcohol base, and the standard "fifth" bottle contains 25.6 ounces. Three cups of base equals 24 ounces, and if you buy it by the half-gallon, three cups will suffice for a fifth in any of these recipes. As the saying goes, "That's close enough for government work."

If you want to make a lesser amount of liqueur than these recipes yield, the easiest way is to reduce the ingredients to one third the amount called for. Thus a recipe that called for a fifth of vodka and a cup of sweetening would be reduced to one cup of vodka and one-third cup of sugar syrup.

Sweetening

Most homemade liqueurs are sweetened with a sugar syrup made by boiling one cup of sugar with one-half cup of water for several minutes. This makes one cup of sugar syrup, and in general one cup is sufficient to sweeten one fifth (about 25 ounces) alcohol base for a medium-sweet liqueur. Two cups sugar syrup per fifth are required for very sweet crème-type liqueurs.

Most frequently, ordinary white sugar is used for liqueurs, but interesting variations can be obtained with honey, light-brown sugar, or unrefined raw sugar. In addition to the flavor they add, these alternatives to white sugar have a higher nutritive value, especially in regard to minerals. (Experiments have demonstrated that rats fed a diet of white sugar develop more cavities than those fed brown sugar or honey.) Although I am not an extreme health food faddist, I have switched from sugar to honey for sweetening many of my own liqueurs, but mainly because the flavor and smoothness are superior when honey is used.

Honey does have a drawback in liqueurs in that it imparts a cloudiness to drinks which, unless removed, makes them less attractive to the eye than are liqueurs made with sugar syrup. Directions for removing the cloudiness are given on page 32. The process essentially involves letting the mixed liqueur sit for a month or so until the cloudiness settles out and then siphoning off the clear portion.

If you decide to use honey, choose a light-colored, mild honey such as clover. Some of the dark honeys such as wildflower and blackberry have a very strong flavor that can distort or overwhelm the flavor of your liqueur. Some exceptionally smooth imported honeys, such as heather, are more expensive than domestic clover honey but are worth the price in special cases. When substituting honey for sugar syrup, I simply use a cup of honey in place of a cup of sugar syrup.

Water

Some prefer to use only distilled water in making the syrup to sweeten their liqueurs and for diluting them to the proper strength when grain neutral spirits have been used for the alcohol base. I consider the use of distilled water an unnecessary precaution, but I do believe that it is important to boil the water for a few minutes and let it cool to room temperature before using. The purpose of this is to boil off the chlorine that is often present in drinking water. Chlorine produces chemical reactions that will cause some of the subtle flavorings and aromatic oils to break down. Although this does not destroy the liqueur completely, it does lead to a less flavorful and less aromatic drink than if you first boil the water and drive off the chlorine.

Glycerine

Commercial producers of liqueurs invariably add glycerine to their products to increase their "body," that is, give them a thicker consistency and make them heavier. Glycerine, which can be purchased in any drugstore, is a product which is derived from fat and also occurs naturally in the body. Some home liqueurmakers who wish to limit their intake of fat and fat by-products do not include it, but you only need one teaspoon per quart of finished liqueur to give your beverages a nice consistency, and it is doubtful that this small amount of glycerine would be harmful in any way.

Coloring

The use of food coloring to give your beverages a pleasing color is also something that many of those who are committed to health foods balk at. However, the only food color which has been seriously questioned as being possibly detrimental to health is red. The other colors have an untarnished reputation, and in any case only a very few drops are needed to color a quart of liqueur. Red commercial food coloring is the only one which I do not use myself. If you are a purist, there are natural means of getting some colors. Dried nettle or spinach leaves are a good source of green color if added to material steeping in alcohol, and although it is expensive, a tiny pinch of saffron imparts a rich golden shade of yellow.

Flavoring

Flavorings for liqueurs are usually substances of plant origin such as herbs, spices, fruit, nuts, beans, and flower petals. Some liqueurs have chemically produced flavorings; and occasionally substances such as amber, musk, and gold or silver flakes are added. A few of the recipes in this book call for flavoring extracts, but only when these extracts are derived from the plant itself.

Whenever possible I use only pure fruit or herbs and spices in liqueurmaking. In liqueurs the flavor is almost always superior when natural rather than chemical artificial flavors are used. The use of natural products also gives one a more secure feeling when drinking the liqueur. Fruits free of insecticide are always preferable, and they are usually available in health food stores.

Most of the herbs and spices required can usually be obtained in either a supermarket or a health food store. See page 38 for a list of vendors who sell by mail order. Freshly ground spices are usually more aromatic than commercially ground ones, so you may wish to grind them yourself when possible. Leftover herbs and spices should be kept in tightly closed jars, preferably in a cool place, to retain their flavor.

Most of the herbs called for in these recipes make pleasant teas which you may want to try, rather than discarding leftover material after making liqueurs. A general rule for herb tea is to use one teaspoon per cup and brew ten minutes. Sweeten with honey.

Filtering with cloth

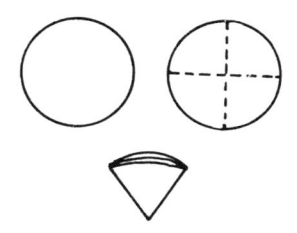

Filtering with filter paper

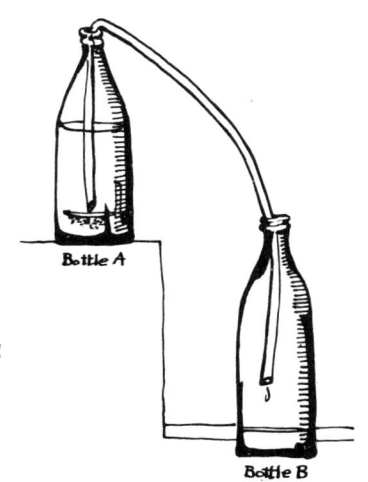

Siphoning

Bottle A

Bottle B

CLARIFYING

Most of the time you can get clear homemade liqueurs by filtering through cloth several times and having the last filtration go through several layers of cloth. Although some French sources recommend silk, I have always obtained good results with clean cotton. First remove as many fruit or herb particles as possible by pouring through a wire strainer. It is best to begin filtering with a fairly coarse weave such as cheesecloth and then progress to a tighter weave. Use a piece of cloth considerably larger than the top of the jar you are filtering into so that you can shift the cloth over to a clear area if the pores clog. In a series of three or four filterings you should end by using a tight weave of cotton folded in three or more layers. If you try to do all this in one step, the pores of the cloth will clog and the filtering will take a long time. This is a mistake because the alcohol strength of your liqueur will decrease from the evaporation while it is exposed to the air for this long period.

For filtering fruit liqueurs it is useful to sew the cloth into the form of a bag, such as the jelly bags used by those who make their own jellies and jams, so that the fruit pulp can be squeezed and wrung. This enables you to extract more alcohol and flavor from the fruit.

To filter homemade liqueur with filter paper, use the most porous, or "fastest," paper that you can find. This can usually be obtained in chemical-supply houses and most hobby shops. It helps to pour the infusion of alcohol base and flavoring material through a wire strainer first so that the pores of the paper do not clog so quickly. To filter, fold the circle of paper into quarters, spread it into a little cone, and then insert it into a funnel. When filtering, do not let the level of the liquid go above the top of the paper. As the pores of the paper clog, the filtering takes longer; change the paper when clogging becomes excessive.

Sometimes a faint cloudiness will remain after filtering. If the

Brooklin Concrete Products
LIMITED

1 recipe condensed milk
whiskey or scotch
whipping cream

Fresh orange liqueur
4 large oranges
¼ cup granulated sugar
1 (25 oz.) bottle alcohol

Carefully remove the peel from the oranges. If there is any white pithy part left on the peel, scrape it off. Otherwise you'll have a bitter taste.

Put the peel in a large jar and sprinkle with sugar. Add the alcohol. Cover and store in a cool place for about six weeks. Shake the jar occasionally. Pour the liquid off, strain and bottle. You may want to add a touch of cognac for smoothness.

Makes about 3 cups.

joe syrup
coconut extract
powder till
will keep for
3 weeks

4 LOCATIONS TO SERVE YOU:
HIGHWAY 12, BROOKLIN, ONT. • (416) 655-3311
YONGE ST., NEWMARKET, ONT. • (416) 895-2373
HIGHWAY 11, HUNTSVILLE, ONT. • (705) 789-2338
HIGHWAY 121, HALIBURTON, ONT. • (705) 457-1395

Xmas 1979

Paul Masson Brandy + 2½ tsp Orange Extract

Xmas 1980

LCBO French Brandy + 3 tsp Orange Extract

Xmas 1981

D'EAUBONNE Brandy +

Brooklin Concrete Products
LIMITED

4 LOCATIONS TO SERVE YOU:
HIGHWAY 12, BROOKLIN, ONT. • (416) 655-3311
YONGE ST., NEWMARKET, ONT. • (416) 895-2373
HIGHWAY 11, HUNTSVILLE, ONT. • (705) 789-2338
HIGHWAY 121, HALIBURTON, ONT. • (705) 457-1395

cloudiness is not due to honey, you can frequently obtain the clarity of commercially made liqueurs by letting the product sit for several weeks. Siphoning is the best method of clarifying liqueurs which have been sweetened with honey. Let the bottle of sweetened liqueur stand undisturbed until all the sediment, such as pollen particles, settles to the bottom. This takes a month or two, depending on the degree of cloudiness. Uncap the bottle without disturbing it, and insert a plastic tube to within half an inch of the sediment. Suck on the other end of the tube for a moment. When the liquid starts to flow, insert the tube into a second bottle that is on a lower level, and the contents will flow through the tube. Corks with holes drilled into them, such as the kind used in chemistry labs, are useful for holding the tube in place. Try to get as much of the clear liqueur and avoid as much of the sediment as possible. Incidentally, although it does not look good, the remaining liqueur with the sediment is not harmful and tastes fine, since the sediment is mainly pollen from the honey. There is no reason why you should not take a drink from the remains at this point for a reward to yourself.

There are other methods of clarifying liqueurs that involve adding substances which precipitate to the bottom and take the cloudy material with them, so that the clear liqueur can be easily decanted off. Two such substances are egg white and alum. I do not use these in my own liqueurmaking, as I have always been able to get satisfactory results by filtering and siphoning (except for chocolate-flavored liqueurs, and that is a special case anyway). Furthermore, the egg white and alum techniques do not always work. However, since they often do, they will be presented here for the sake of completeness.

Powdered alum can be obtained in a drugstore. The correct amount to add is a teaspoon and a half per quart of finished liqueur. Add the alum and shake well. The alum will precipitate to the bottom, taking the cloudiness with it. The clear liqueur can then be decanted off and the remainder filtered clear with filter paper. Since the process does not always work and sometimes too many of the substances which impart the flavor are also removed, it is important to test it on a small amount first. One-half teaspoon of alum to ten ounces of liqueur seems to be good for trials. Alum is not a harmful substance, and you will not hurt yourself if you accidentally ingest some of it in trying this process, but you should try to remove all of it by filtering and decanting, since it has a rather astringent taste.

The process with egg white is the same as with alum, although I do not think it works as well. Try a half-teaspoon of egg white per quart of liqueur as a start. If it does not work, most of it can be removed by filtering and any remaining amount causes no problems. Henley's *20th Century Formulas* states that liqueurs can be clarified with talcum in the same manner as with alum. I have not tried this procedure, as I have a general reluctance to use any of these clarifying agents in my own liqueurs. I feel better drinking them when I know they contain no additives, only pure fruit, herbs, spices, sugar, or honey.

LABELING AND KEEPING A LOG

Although it may seem trivial it really is important to put labels on the bottles in which you have liqueurs steeping and to keep

A log for liqueurmaking records

General Considerations and Directions 35

a notebook for writing down the ingredients you have used and also the dates and length of time that you put things in to steep. I have often had the experience of having a liqueur come out really good but then had trouble duplicating it. Taste will tell you what the ingredients are, but quantities and steeping times are hard to remember.

Entries in a Notebook or Log for Liqueurmaking

MATERIALS USED:

INGREDIENTS	AMOUNT
_____	_____
_____	_____
_____	_____
_____	_____
_____	_____

Alcohol Base: Proof:

Date Mixed:

Date Filtered:

Type of Filtering:

Date Sweetened:

Sweetening Used:

Comments:

3

Recipes for Liqueurs Flavored with Herbs and Spices

Herb and spice liqueurs are the most interesting and also the easiest to make. Their preparation is almost as simple as brewing a pot of tea. You simply steep the herbs in an alcohol base for the required amount of time, filter, and sweeten. Except for a few herbs that have an unusually bitter taste or a high natural sugar content, the sweetening process is also simple in that a standard amount of sugar syrup or honey is added to the alcohol base in order to achieve a given degree of sweetness. With fruit liqueurs this process is much less simple because the various types of fruit have different amounts of natural sugar content.

The many different flavorful and aromatic herbs in existence add to the interest, since the various combinations of these make for an almost endless variety of possible flavors. Botanists restrict the term "herb" to those plants that do not have woody parts. The more common and loose definition of the term as any plant material that is used for flavor, aroma, or medicinal value is the one employed in this book. Most of the finer and more popular commercially made liqueurs are flavored with herbs. Examples are Benedictine, Chartreuse, Drambuie, Galliano, Irish Mist, Strega, and crème de menthe.

The background of these and other herb-flavored liqueurs makes for fascinating study. The history of herb liqueurs is associated both with early medicine and with witchcraft. Since the shamans and witches of pre-Christian Europe performed the functions of both healer and sorcerer, these subjects became interrelated. Considerable herbal lore was accumulated by these people, and after the technique for distilling alcohol was developed, herbs were infused to produce remedies, love potions, and the like.

We should not be too scornful of ancient beliefs concerning herbs, because many of them have a solid basis vindicated by science. A 1962 survey of more than 300 million new prescriptions written in the United States showed that 25 percent were for drugs from natural plant materials.[1] Many of the remaining 75 percent were for drugs produced by the chemical industry from ingredients that were originally found in plants but later synthesized and produced from chemicals. Physicians tend to prescribe these synthetic drugs because dosage can be controlled somewhat better than when the natural plant is used. Many herbal remedies do work in a direct way, and many others work for indirect reasons. As Euell Gibbons has pointed out in his excellent book *Stalking the Healthful Herbs*, a number of herbs are quite rich in vitamins and minerals, and thus many of the claims made by herbalists for medicinal values may be attributed to the relief of vitamin-deficiency diseases. In addition, some herbs, such as wormwood, act as a vermifuge and expel parasites from the body, and many others, such as thyme, have strong antibacterial properties. It may be that certain herb blends and combinations became known as love potions because individuals who had been too debilitated from parasites and vitamin deficiency to maintain an active sex life could perform after being treated with infusions of herbs prepared by a village crone who was credited with occult powers for producing these "cures."

1. Arnold Krochmal et al., *A Guide to Medicinal Plants of Appalachia*, U.S. Department of Agriculture Handbook 400 (Washington, D.C., 1971), p. 1.

Even through the European Renaissance herbal liqueurs were associated with a weird blend of science and occultism. It is only in comparatively recent times that medicine and botany became sciences free from superstitious lore, and it is also true that until the past three hundred or so years, distillers were frequently alchemists and magicians on the side. Regardless of this background, however, the best reason for using herb-flavored liqueurs today is their splendid flavor and aroma.

The recipes in this chapter are based on dried rather than freshly collected herbs. Fresh herbs contain moisture and you must use much more to obtain the same strength. I do not recommend that you collect the herbs yourself unless you are an expert, since many of those in the fields and woods are toxic. Most health food stores stock herbs, and many of those called for in these recipes (for example, allspice berries, caraway seed, celery seed, coriander, cinnamon, ginger, rosemary, and vanilla bean) can be found in the spice section of supermarkets. If you do not live near a health food store that stocks herbs, three vendors who sell by mail order are:

>Aphrodisia Products, Inc.
>28 Carmine Street
>New York, New York 10014

This firm has an extensive selection, and it is the only place I know of that stocks zebrovka. Their catalog has a lot of herbal lore, and it is worth the price of 50 cents.

>Meadowbrook Herb Garden
>Wyoming, Rhode Island 02898

This company has very high-quality herbs, most of which they grow themselves without insecticides or artificial fertilizer. They make the Coltea blend called for in one of the recipes. Their catalog costs 50 cents. Unfortunately the number of herbs they stock is somewhat lower than that of the other vendors mentioned.

>Wide World of Herbs, Ltd.
>11 Saint Catherine St. East
>Montreal 129, Canada

Liqueurs Flavored with Herbs and Spices

This is one of the largest herb companies in North America. They stock more than 2,000 herbs and botanicals. Their price list is free, although they require a minimum order of $5.00. For a small additional fee your order is mailed to you from within the United States so you do not have to wait a long time for it to clear customs.

Using herbs and spices to make liqueurs is relatively easy, but there are a few precautions that you should take. Although dried herbs and spices do not spoil, their aromatic oils evaporate over time and they become bland. They will keep longer if kept in tightly closed jars. This is also true when they are steeping in alcohol; you do not want your alcohol content lowered by evaporation.

Many herbs must be crushed or at least bruised so that their flavor and aroma are released. This is especially true of herbs and spices in the form of a hard seed like anise or fennel or a dried berry like allspice. Although some of these substances can be purchased already ground, the flavor of freshly ground material is far better, whether one is making liqueurs or cooking. Comparing commercially ground pepper with some that you grind yourself will illustrate this. A mortar and pestle provide the best way of crushing herbs and spices. Just work them until the desired fine or coarse grind is achieved. If you do not have

Crushing herbs for liqueurmaking

a mortar, you can spread the material out on a cutting board and press it with the back of a spoon. For grinding really hard material, such as cherry stones, wrap it in cloth and pound with a hammer.

The recipes in this chapter present only a few of the vast number of liqueurs that can be made with herbs. Many hundreds of herb-flavored liqueurs are made throughout the world with all sorts of botanicals. In parts of Asia a liqueur-type drink is made by infusing marijuana in alcohol. If you wish to go beyond the recipes presented here and experiment with other herbs and combinations of them, there are two general rules. First, start with small amounts of herbs. If your drink comes out too mild in flavor, more can always be added to strengthen it, but not much can be done with something overpowering in taste. Second, in general, barks, seeds, and roots require longer steeping times than leaves or flower petals.

The recipes presented in this section were chosen because they are generally well liked, and I think that they all taste good except for those containing wormwood. That is one taste I have not been able to acquire, but I included recipes using it because of the mystique and folklore surrounding it. My guests are always eager to try it, but I do not get requests for seconds. My own taste preferences, which are presented as a guide and not in the belief that you will necessarily agree with me, are: angelica, especially number 4, star anise, kümmel, celery seed number 2, mint, rosemary, and the Coltea blend. Those which I prefer least are those with wormwood, juniper berry, orris root, and tonka bean.

Allspice Cordial

Everyone is familiar with the use of allspice as a condiment, but it is not widely known that a very pleasant and warming cordial can be made from allspice berries. Allspice is indigenous to the West Indies and South America. It was unknown in Europe

Liqueurs Flavored with Herbs and Spices

until after the voyages of Christopher Columbus, who reputedly was responsible for introducing it there. Spice experts state that the best allspice comes from Jamaica, where the trees reach a height of about 30 feet. It was given the name allspice because the flavor suggests a blend of several spices including cloves, cinnamon, and nutmeg. Medicinal benefits have been attributed to allspice for a carminative action in the gastrointestinal tract, and an allspice paste was formerly used as a counterirritant for the pains of neuralgia and rheumatism. It was once listed in the U.S. Pharmacopoeia for these purposes but has since been dropped. It is advisable to get allspice berries for the following recipe and crush them yourself rather than to buy ground allspice, because the aroma is better.

- 3 teaspoons freshly ground allspice
- 1 fifth vodka
- 1 cup sugar syrup

Let the allspice steep in the vodka for a week, and then strain through clean cloth, add the sweetening, and bottle. This makes a very aromatic and warming cordial that is especially pleasant on a cold winter day.

ANGELICA-BASED LIQUEURS

Angelica is probably the most important herb flavoring in the better-known commercial liqueurs. Benedictine, yellow and green Chartreuse, Drambuie, Galliano, and Strega all contain angelica among their unique combinations of botanical ingredients. This herb grows widely throughout Europe in cool and moist places from northern Scandinavia to the Pyrenees. The herb has been used since ancient times, and it has a prominent place in folklore. Pagan festivals were associated with it, and it was long considered efficacious against spells and enchantments. In modern times its purposes have been somewhat more mundane. It is used as a flavoring; the candied stalks are used as a confection; and the leaves are smoked by Laplanders. Herbalists hold the plant in high esteem for its medicinal value. They believe that it is useful as a general tonic, an aid in bronchitis, and a remedy for indigestion. Although I am not sure about the first two claims, it certainly is a good digestive aid either as a tea or in a liqueur. It rapidly dispels nausea, especially from overeating. The entire plant is aromatic, and the leaves, seeds, stems, or roots can be used. Since the chopped root is the form most commonly available in the United States, I have developed these recipes around that form. These recipes will produce close simulations of their commercial counterparts, but the taste will not be exactly the same. The recipes of the commercial brands are closely guarded secrets known only to a very few individuals, and when they are written they are stored in bank vaults. Although I like all of these liqueurs, my favorites are numbers 2 and 4. Benedictine and green Chartreuse also contain angelica, but I have not yet been able to develop close simulations. I have used SeeLect brand angelica root, which is available in most health food stores.

Angelica Liqueur Number 1
(A Simulation of Yellow Chartreuse)

- 1½ teaspoons chopped angelica root
- 3 teaspoons melissa (sometimes called balm, or lemon balm)
- 3 teaspoons hyssop
- 3-inch cinnamon stick
- Scant ¼ teaspoon mace
- 1 fifth vodka
- 1 cup sugar syrup
- Pinch of saffron or yellow food coloring (optional)

Liqueurs Flavored with Herbs and Spices

Combine all ingredients except for sugar syrup in a large jar, close tightly, and shake well. Let the ingredients steep for one week, and filter through cloth several times. Add the sugar syrup, and the liqueur is ready. You may want to add a tiny pinch of saffron or a little yellow food coloring to get a deep-yellow color.

Angelica Liqueur Number 2 (A Simulation of Drambuie)

- 1½ teaspoons chopped angelica root
- 1 fifth Scotch whiskey
- 1 cup honey

Add the angelica to the Scotch and let it steep only overnight. This is important because only a delicate hint of angelica is called for in this recipe, and the flavor will be too strong if it is allowed to steep longer. Strain the angelica out and add the honey. The liqueur will taste fine at this point, but it will have an undesirable cloudiness. If you let it set undisturbed for two months, all the cloudiness will settle out and you can siphon off a sparkling clear liqueur with a golden color. This is a delicious liqueur and one of my favorites.

Angelica Liqueur Number 3 (A Simulation of Galliano)

- 3 teaspoons chopped angelica root
- 3-inch cinnamon stick
- 1 clove
- Scant ¼ teaspoon freshly ground nutmeg
- Scant ¼ teaspoon mace
- 1 fifth vodka
- 1 cup sugar syrup

Proceed as in the directions for Angelica Liqueur Number 1. This is a slightly similar liqueur but a good deal more spicy. It is very good and may be used in any cocktail recipe that calls for Galliano.

Angelica Liqueur Number 4 (A Simulation of Strega)

- 6 cardamom pods
- 3 teaspoons anise seed
- 2¼ teaspoons chopped angelica root
- 1 three-inch cinnamon stick
- 1 clove
- Scant ¼ teaspoon mace
- 1 fifth vodka
- 1 cup sugar syrup

Remove the cardamom seeds from the pods, discard pods and crush seeds in a mortar. The anise seeds should also be worked for a few minutes in the mortar. Then combine the ingredients, except for the sweetening, in a large jar. Shake well, close tightly, and let steep for one week. Strain the materials out, and filter through cloth several times. Sweeten, and the liqueur is ready to drink. This is an excellent liqueur, and it can be even better if honey is used instead of sugar and it is clarified by siphoning as in the directions for Angelica Liqueur Number 2.

ANISE, FENNEL, AND LICORICE LIQUEURS

Anise, fennel, star anise, and licorice are spices with similar flavors, and all are used in liqueurmaking. Anise is the most widely used, both as a main ingredient and as an ancillary flavor as in absinthe. It is one of the oldest spices, having been in use

Liqueurs Flavored with Herbs and Spices

since Egyptian times as a medicine and flavoring. At various periods in history it was considered to have magical properties such as the ability to protect one from the evil eye. Fennel seed has a similar appearance and taste, although it is milder than anise seed. Nicholas Culpepper, the famed seventeenth-century herbalist whose work contains such an odd mixture of solid information and nonsense, believed that fennel-seed tea was an aid in weight reduction. Licorice root is similar to anise and fennel in flavor. It differs from them in that it is sweet at first but has a bitter and sharp aftertaste. Star anise, a completely different plant from regular anise, is the dried fruit of a small evergreen tree found in China. (It is sometimes called Chinese anise.) It is relatively difficult to find in the United States, although herb dealers sometimes have it, as do many Chinese groceries in the larger cities, where it is called *pa-chao*.

All of these substances have similar medicinal properties in that they have a carminative effect on the stomach, sweeten bad breath, and are a good expectorant for coughs, as their wide use in cough drops and lozenges indicates. Most of the commercially made liqueurs with these flavors are rather sweet except for the Spanish-made liqueur Anis del Mono.

Anise Liqueur or Anisette

- 2 tablespoons anise seed
- 1½ teaspoons fennel seed
- 1½ teaspoons ground coriander
- 1 fifth vodka
- 1–2 cups sugar syrup, according to taste

If the anise and fennel seed are first worked in a mortar, the flavor will be a little stronger. Add the spices to the vodka, and let them steep for one week. Shake the jar occasionally during the week, and then strain the material through cloth several times. Add one cup of sugar syrup, stir, and taste. I like it at this point, although many prefer a sweeter drink like commercial anisette. If you prefer it sweeter, take another cup of sugar syrup and add a little at a time, stirring and tasting as you go. Do not exceed two cups of syrup.

Licorice Liqueur or Raki

- 3 tablespoons chopped licorice root
- 1 fifth vodka
- 6 ounces sugar syrup

I do not like this liqueur as well as the ones based on anise or star anise, but raki is a very popular drink in the Eastern Mediterranean countries, especially Turkey, where it is sometimes used without sweetening. Let the chopped licorice root marinate in the vodka for one week, and then strain it out and sweeten. The aftertaste is somewhat bitter at first but improves a little when the mixture has been aged about three months.

Star Anise Liqueur

- 2 tablespoons broken and slightly crushed star anise
- 1 fifth vodka
- 1–2 cups sugar syrup, according to taste

Put the lightly crushed star anise, which has been worked in a mortar for a few minutes, into the vodka to steep for a week

Liqueurs Flavored with Herbs and Spices

and a half. Then filter out the star anise and add one cup of sugar syrup. Stir and taste, then add more syrup until it suits your preference. This is a very aromatic drink with a pleasant taste. A nice visual effect can be obtained if you have a relatively clear decanter with a mouth a little wider than most liqueur bottles. After the liqueur is finished, take a small but intact anise star, rinse it lightly in warm water, and add it to the bottle. The pretty seven-pointed star will float just below the surface.

DRINKS FLAVORED WITH CARAWAY SEED

Americans are familiar with the flavor of caraway seed from the sharp and spicy taste that it gives to rye bread. In northern Europe these seeds are widely used to flavor various alcoholic drinks. Aquavit, a very popular drink in Scandinavian countries, is flavored with caraway. Since aquavit is not sweetened, it is not, strictly speaking, a liqueur. However, a recipe for it is included in this book because it is a well-known drink with a caraway flavor. Kümmel is also a popular drink in northern Europe, especially in Germany, the Baltic countries, and Russia. For many generations the finest kümmel was produced in Latvia, but the industry never recovered from wartime devastation, and connoisseurs now consider Gilka kümmel, made in Germany, to be the best. In addition to caraway, kümmel usually contains cumin and fennel. There are numerous variations on the recipe. Danzig, Danzigwasser, and Goldwasser are drinks somewhat similar to kümmel, although they have additional spices and also tiny flecks of gold leaf floating in the liqueur. The practice of adding gold leaf to liqueurs comes from medieval times, when it was used as a folk remedy for many ailments, especially rheumatism and arthritis.

Aquavit

    3 slightly rounded teaspoons caraway seed
    1 fifth good vodka

If you have a mortar and pestle, work the caraway seed in the mortar for a few minutes. The seed only has to be cracked a little so that its flavor spreads into the alcohol more easily. If you don't have a mortar, spread the seed out on a bread board and go over it with the bottom of a spoon. Add the seed to the vodka and shake well. Let stand for two weeks in a warm but not hot place. At that point strain the seed with a clean cloth. If a lot of small seed particles still remain, use filter paper.

At this point your aquavit is ready. It will have a slight brownish color, which is due to the caraway. Most commercial aquavit is clear, because the oil of caraway is extracted from the seeds before adding them, or sometimes the whole solution is redistilled after the caraway has been marinated. The taste, however, will be the same as Scandinavian aquavits. Aquavit is typically served straight and very cold. It is an excellent accompaniment to hors d'oeuvre.

Caraway Cordial

    3 level tablespoons caraway seed
    1 fifth vodka
    1 cup sugar syrup

Add the caraway seed to the vodka, and let steep for two

weeks. At that point strain out the seeds and add the sugar syrup.

This is a tasty but sharp and piquant liqueur. If a less piquant liqueur is desired, decrease the caraway seed to 2 tablespoons. An interesting variation is to use 1½ cups brandy and 1½ cups vodka for the alcohol base.

Kümmel

  2 level tablespoons caraway seed
  3 teaspoons fennel seed
  1½ teaspoons powdered cumin
  1 fifth vodka
  1 cup sugar syrup

Work the caraway and fennel seeds in a mortar with a pestle for a few minutes or press them with the back of a spoon on a bread board before adding them and the cumin to the vodka. The seeds and cumin should marinate in the vodka for a week and a half. At that point strain them out with a wire strainer or clean cloth. If the solution still has a lot of debris in it, filter with filter paper. Add the sugar syrup, and your kümmel is ready to serve.

There are numerous variations on the kümmel formula, although the recipe given above compares with the best imported kümmels. If you are the type who likes to experiment, however, you may wish to try some of the variations. Allash kümmel is a very sweet variety that contains a touch of almond in addition to caraway. Another variation is to use orris root in place of the cumin, and many people like to add a small amount of lemon or orange peel to the solution while it is marinating.

Danzig and Goldwasser

    2 level tablespoons caraway seed
    2 teaspoons anise seed
    ⅓ teaspoon ground coriander
    1 three-inch cinnamon stick
    1 piece of lemon peel
    1½ cloves
    1 fifth vodka
    1 cup sugar syrup
    A small amount of tiny gold flecks (optional)

Prepare like kümmel in preceding recipe. Let the spices steep in the vodka for a week and a half, then strain through cloth and sweeten. If you can get the gold leaf, it adds a nice visual effect when the bottle is shaken, but it is doubtful that the medicinal effects attributed to it by folklore are valid, since gold is rather inert chemically and most likely simply passes through the system.

CELERY CORDIALS

Celery is familiar to people in the United States as an aromatic vegetable. In Europe the plant is put to a greater variety of uses. The leaves as well as the stalks are more often added to soups and salads, and the roots of some varieties are commonly used as a vegetable known as celeriac. In France a rather good cordial known as crème de celery is made from the seeds. Two recipes for crème de celery are given in this section. Although I like both, I definitely prefer the second.

Liqueurs Flavored with Herbs and Spices

Celery Cordial Number 1
 1 tablespoon celery seed
 1 fifth vodka
 1–2 cups sugar syrup

Crush the celery seed in a mortar or on a board with the back of a spoon. Add to the vodka, and let steep for six days. Then filter through cloth and sweeten. I prefer to use just one cup of sugar syrup with this recipe, but people who like very sweet crème-type liqueurs may wish to add two.

Celery Cordial Number 2
 1 tablespoon celery seed
 2 teaspoons caraway seed
 ¾ teaspoon fennel seed
 1 fifth vodka
 1–2 cups sugar syrup

Crush the seeds a little by working with a mortar, and let them steep in the vodka for six days. Filter through clean cotton cloth, then sweeten. This cordial tastes best to me when sweetened with just one cup of sugar syrup, although it has a sugar content more like two when made commercially in France.

❖

Cinnamon and Coriander Cordial

Cinnamon and coriander are two well-known spices, found in most grocery stores, that can be used to make a very tasty and aromatic cordial. You are probably familiar with the aroma and flavor of the reddish-brown cinnamon that has been a major commodity in the spice trade for centuries. There is another variety called Ceylon cinnamon which is tan in color and milder in flavor. The standard red-brown variety is the one used in the following recipe. Coriander, which is a member of the carrot family, has been used since ancient times, although it has become somewhat less popular in recent years. It has a very interesting flavor that suggests a blend of anise and citrus fruit peel. A combination of brandy and vodka is used in this recipe because the brandy contributes to flavor, but the flavor becomes too powerful when only brandy is used.

- 1 three- to four-inch cinnamon stick
- 1 level tablespoon ground coriander
- 1½ cups vodka
- 1½ cups brandy
- 1 cup sugar syrup

Let the cinnamon stick and coriander steep for a week in the vodka and brandy. Strain well through cloth, and add the syrup to sweeten. This is a very pleasant cordial, and if you are the type that enjoys experimenting with recipes, a number of variations are possible. Many people like to add a clove or two as well as some cardamom seeds or some lemon peel.

Damiana Liqueur

Damiana is a small shrub that grows in the southwestern United States and also in Mexico. Among the Indians of northwestern Mexico it is reputed to be an aphrodisiac, and many herbalists agree with this claim. Even Mrs. M. Grieve, undoubtedly among the most knowledgeable of modern herbalists, who rarely makes a claim for any herb unless it has solid scientific backing, states

Liqueurs Flavored with Herbs and Spices

that damiana has an aphrodisiac effect. It seems to me, however, that with this particular herb any such effect is a placebo one; that is, it works because people expect it to work.

Whether or not damiana is aphrodisiacal, an interesting liqueur can be made from the plant. Such a liqueur is made commercially in Mexico and is simply called Damiana. It is imported into the United States by Paddington Corporation and sold in attractive bottles in those liquor stores that stock a large variety of liqueurs and cordials.

2½ tablespoons crumbled damiana
1 fifth vodka
1 cup sugar syrup or honey

Steep the damiana in the vodka for one week, then strain and filter. Sweeten with sugar syrup or honey if you prefer.

Damiana has a strong aromatic herbal scent slightly reminiscent of sage or thyme. If you find this unpleasant, you may want to add some anise seed to change the aroma. Add a couple of teaspoons at a time, letting the mixture steep for a week each time, until you find a combination that pleases you. Your leftover damiana may be brewed into a tea, one teaspoon per cup steeped for ten minutes, or it may be smoked.

GINGER CORDIALS

Ginger-flavored cordials make spicy and piquant drinks that were somewhat more popular in former years than currently. Colonial Americans believed that they were a remedy for colds and sore throats. Although there is no scientific evidence to support that belief, the ginger does have a carminative effect, and these cordials are very pleasant after a meal or in cold weather.

Ginger Cordial Number 1

    ¾ teaspoon ground ginger
    1 fifth brandy
    1½ cups sugar syrup or honey

Add the ginger to the brandy, and shake well. Let the mixture steep for six days, and then filter with clean cotton cloth. The filtering is a little difficult because the woody particles in the ginger tend to clog the cloth so that you have to shift it over a little to a clean area. I like to use honey with ginger because the flavors go well together. If you use honey rather than sugar syrup to sweeten, shake well, let it stand for another three weeks, and then siphon off the clear liquid.

Ginger Cordial Number 2

    ¾ teaspoons ground ginger
    2 cloves
    2 cardamoms (discard the pods and use only seeds)
    ⅓ teaspoon cinnamon
    1 fifth brandy
    1½ cups sugar syrup or honey

Add the spices to the brandy, and make as in the preceding recipe. This is a somewhat more tasty and spicy drink than the first, although both are really quite agreeable. Some other variations on ginger cordial are to add pepper to increase the piquancy, or to add mace and vanilla.

Juniper Berry Cordial

Juniper berries, which give gin its characteristic flavor, can also be used as the main flavor in a liqueur. The flavor is not quite the same as in gin because that contains other botanicals in addition to juniper. The berries alone have a more balsamlike flavor, and the aroma is slightly like that of a cedar chest. In some areas these berries are also used to flavor meat, especially game.

- 1 tablespoon (about 6 dozen) dried juniper berries
- 1 fifth brandy
- 1/3 slightly rounded teaspoon ground coriander
- 1 cup sugar syrup

Crush the juniper berries (they do not have to be ground to a powder, but they should at least be broken), and add them to the brandy. Add the coriander, and shake well. Let steep for two weeks, and then strain through cotton cloth. Sweeten with the sugar syrup, and it's ready to serve. This is not really one of my favorite cordials—this does not surprise me because I do not like drinks made with gin very much either—but many people do like it.

Lovage Liqueur

A very pleasant cordial that is warm and aromatic can be made from lovage, which is seldom seen as a culinary herb today but was widely used in previous generations. In English pubs lovage cordial was a very popular item prior to the First World War, but I know of no commercial firm that makes it now. A cordial can be made with lovage leaves, seeds, or root. The tastes of all three are quite similar, but the root is difficult to obtain and the seeds require a long steeping time, so I use the leaves. Chopped leaves of excellent quality are marketed as an herb seasoning by the Meadowbrook Herb Garden (see page 38).

    1½ tablespoons chopped lovage
    1 fifth brandy
    1 cup sugar syrup

Put the lovage and the brandy in a jar, close tightly, and shake well. Let the mixture steep for one week, and then strain through cloth and sweeten. The result is an easy-to-make but delicious liqueur.

Melissa, or Lemon Balm, Liqueur

Melissa, also known as balm, sweet balm, and lemon balm, is extensively used in liqueurmaking, both alone and in combination with other herbs. This herb is a different plant from the balm of Gilead referred to in the Bible, but it does have a long history of use in teas and as a flavoring for wines. In Roman times it was used as a dressing for wounds. According to M. Grieve, there is a sound scientific basis for this practice because melissa does have an antibacterial action. A number of commercially made liqueurs contain melissa, and the recipe for simulating yellow Chartreuse given in the section on angelica has melissa as one of its ingredients. The following recipe based on melissa alone produces a sweet-tasting liqueur with a mild herbal flavor.

    3 tablespoons dried melissa
    1 fifth brandy
    1 cup sugar syrup

Liqueurs Flavored with Herbs and Spices

This herb needs to be steeped in the brandy for 24 hours only, and then filtered and sweetened. Because of the herb's natural sweetness, this liqueur is somewhat sweeter than most other liqueurs, although it has only one cup of sugar syrup per fifth of alcohol base. It is a pleasant liqueur to have with coffee at the end of a meal.

MINT LIQUEURS AND CORDIALS

Since mint is the most widely used of all herbs, it is not surprising that crème de menthe is one of the most popular cordials. Although there are many varieties of mint, spearmint and peppermint are by far the most widely used. Peppermint is an excellent remedy for nausea. Herbalists believe that it is also effective against flatulence and diarrhea and that it relieves stomach cramps because of an antispasmodic action. Spearmint has a carminative action that is similar to but less effective than that of peppermint.

The recipes below provide for both natural leaf and mint extract. Do not use synthetic oil of peppermint or peppermint spirit; they simply do not make nearly so good a drink as natural extract. However, I do like the results with McCormick's mint flavoring, which is made from a combination of synthetic mint oil and natural extract. Since different brands vary considerably in the strength of their flavor, proceed cautiously if you use a brand different from McCormick's. Add half a teaspoon at a time until you get a good flavor if you are experimenting with a brand of unknown strength. Two cups of sugar will produce about the same sweetness as a commercial crème de menthe, but I use only 1½ cups in mine, since I prefer it less sweet.

Crème de Menthe

- 2¼ teaspoons McCormick's Pure Mint Peppermint Extract
- 1 fifth vodka
- 1½–2 cups sugar syrup
- 1 teaspoon glycerine

Simply combine ingredients in a large jar or bottle and shake well. The liqueur can then be used immediately, but it becomes a little smoother if it stands about two weeks. This recipe makes an excellent crème de menthe, and I like being able to make it less sweet than commercial varieties. Food coloring can be added if you wish to give it a pleasing color. For a really tasty dessert try it as a topping on ice cream.

A crème de menthe type of peppermint cordial can also be made, using dried mint leaves, the same type as used for mint tea.

Peppermint Cordial

- 12 tablespoons dried, well-crumbled peppermint leaves
- 1 fifth vodka
- 1½ cups sugar syrup, or to taste
- 1 teaspoon glycerine

Marinate the mint leaves in the vodka in a large tightly sealed jar for eight days, shaking occasionally. Strain the leaves out,

Liqueurs Flavored with Herbs and Spices

using a metal strainer, and press all the fluid out of the leaves. This step should not be omitted because the material contains considerable flavor. Many small particles of leaves will remain in your alcohol and mint solution at this point. You may just leave them there because the leaves do add a nice effect, but if you are fussy about plant matter in your cordial, strain it through clean cloth. Then add the sweetening and glycerine. The cordial picks up a nice green color from the leaves, so no food coloring is necessary.

A similar cordial can be made with spearmint leaves. It is more fragrant but not as tasty as the peppermint cordial.

Spearmint Cordial

    14 tablespoons dried, well-crumbled spearmint leaves
    1 fifth vodka
   1½ cups sugar syrup
    1 teaspoon glycerine

The procedure for spearmint cordial is the same as that for the preceding peppermint cordial. Since the flavor of spearmint is not as strong as that of peppermint, more of it must be used. It is important that the leaves be well crumbled, or the volume of leaf will be insufficient and the flavor weak. If that happens it can be corrected by adding more leaf and letting it steep.

ORRIS ROOT LIQUEURS

Orris root is actually the root of the Florentine iris. It is widely used in perfumes because of its aroma, which has a resemblance to that of violets. In the Middle Ages it was believed that orris would attract a lover. More recently it was used to treat chronic diarrhea, but it is no longer used in medicine. It is used to flavor cordials and liqueurs both alone and in combination with other botanicals. Of the two recipes below, I prefer the second because the orris alone has pleasant aroma but a bitter component to the taste. Dried orris root is very difficult to grind, but I broke it into pieces a bit smaller than corn kernels for the purpose of measuring in these recipes.

Orris Root Liqueur

> 1 tablespoon pieces of orris root
> 1 fifth vodka or brandy
> 1 cup sugar syrup

Let the orris and vodka or brandy steep for one week in a tightly closed jar, shaking occasionally. Filter through cloth, and sweeten. This liqueur is sometimes a little cloudy, but it can be clarified by letting it stand undisturbed for a couple of months and then siphoning off the clear portion. It also improves somewhat after it stands for a few months.

Orris and Anise Liqueur

> 1 tablespoon pieces of orris root
> 1 tablespoon anise seed
> 1 fifth vodka
> 1 cup sugar syrup

Work the anise in a mortar for a few minutes, and add the orris and anise to the vodka. Put in a tightly closed jar, shake

Liqueurs Flavored with Herbs and Spices 61

occasionally, and after a week filter and sweeten. This liqueur is a beautiful shade of gold, and the aroma is very good, although I do not like the taste of orris so well as that of other botanicals.

ROSEMARY CORDIALS

Rosemary has a warm aromatic scent and, in addition to its culinary uses, provides a source of flavor for two excellent cordials. There is a very rich folklore associated with rosemary that extends from ancient times to the present. It was used at weddings and as a festive decking in churches in earlier centuries, and also as an ingredient in occult rites. In parts of rural Spain and Italy it is still believed to provide protection from witchcraft. Many medicinal effects have been claimed for rosemary. Greek and Roman writers believed that it improved memory. British herbalists have claimed that rosemary boiled in white wine is good for coughs and gout when taken internally and good for scalp and skin disorders applied externally. Although there is probably no scientific evidence to support these claims, the aroma of rosemary alone certainly justifies its use. One of the most delightful smells one can encounter comes on a breeze that blows on a warm day across a field of rosemary gone wild. I still remember very vividly such an experience that I had several years ago while hiking in the foothills near the southern end of the Salinas Valley in California.

Rosemary Cordial Number 1

- ¼ teaspoon bruised rosemary leaves
- 1 fifth Scotch
- 1 cup of honey

This is a delicate cordial with a taste somewhat like Drambuie. It is important that the rosemary be bruised with the back of a spoon on a board so that the aroma is released. Add the rosemary to the Scotch and shake well. Let it stand overnight only, as just a delicate touch of rosemary is best in this cordial, and then strain it out and add the honey. Shake well again and let it stand two to three weeks so that the pollen and other tiny particles in the honey settle out. Then, being careful not to shake the bottle, siphon off the clear portion, which will be all but the last half-inch or so of the bottle.

Rosemary Cordial Number 2

- 1 tablespoon bruised rosemary leaves
- 1 piece of lemon peel (about ¾ inch wide and 6 inches long)
- ¾ teaspoon ground coriander
- 1 fifth vodka
- 1 cup sugar syrup

This recipe makes an excellent cordial that is very warm and aromatic. It is important that the rosemary be bruised to release the aroma. In peeling the lemon, try to get just the outer, yellow portion of the peel and avoid the white inner portion, as it can impart a slight bitter taste. This can be accomplished with a sharp knife or one of the knives made for this purpose with a slot in the blade. Add the rosemary, lemon peel, and coriander to the vodka, shake well, and let steep for a week. Strain well and add the sugar syrup.

TONKA BEAN LIQUEURS

The tonka bean, which comes from a tree found in Brazil and Guiana, has an interesting and exotic aroma that can be used to flavor liqueurs. The aroma is unusual and powerful. Vanilla is the closest to it that I know, but the smell of the tonka bean is sharper and coarser. In addition to being used as a flavoring and in perfumes, a tonka bean is sometimes put into closets or chests to give a pleasant aroma to clothes and linens. Rumona is a commercial liqueur flavored with tonka beans. It is made in Jamaica from tonka beans and fine Jamaican rum. Like many common flavorings such as nutmeg and mace, tonka beans are toxic if the fluid extract is taken in very large doses. They are harmless in the amounts called for in recipes such as these. Of these two recipes I prefer the second.

Tonka Bean Liqueur Number 1

- 1 tonka bean
- 1 fifth vodka
- 1 cup sugar syrup

Let the bean steep in the vodka for two weeks, strain it out, and sweeten. If the flavor is too weak add a fresh bean and test the liqueur after a few days. Steep the second bean for up to two weeks. This procedure will probably be unnecessary, as one average-sized bean will usually do the trick.

Tonka Bean Liqueur Number 2

    1 tonka bean
    1 piece of vanilla bean about 3 inches long
    1 piece of cinnamon stick about 3 to 4 inches long
    1 fifth vodka
    1 cup sugar syrup

Steep the tonka bean, vanilla bean, and cinnamon stick in the vodka for two weeks, then filter and sweeten. Do not oversteep, as the cinnamon will become too strong in relation to the other flavors.

❖

Vanilla Bean Cordial

Vanilla, one of the most popular flavors in the world, can be used to make a smooth and aromatic cordial. Like cacao, vanilla was first cultivated by the Indians of tropical America, although the best vanilla is now reputedly grown on the island of Madagascar. The vanilla pod or bean is actually the fruit of this orchid-bearing plant.

    2–3 vanilla beans (3 if they are shorter than 5 or 6 inches)
    1 fifth vodka
    1 cup sugar syrup

Let the beans steep in the vodka for two weeks, and then take them out. It is unnecessary to filter the solution unless a lot of the small black particles from the interior of the bean have got out into the vodka. Add the sweetening and shake well. This is a very smooth and pleasant cordial, and I am surprised that it is

Liqueurs Flavored with Herbs and Spices 65

not more widely used. It is made commercially in France, but it does not seem to have caught on in other countries.

Verbena, or Lemon Verbena, Cordial

Verbena, or lemon verbena, has a pleasant flavor and lemonlike aroma that makes an excellent cordial. Although the plant originally came from Peru and Chile, it is now widely grown in many areas in Europe and the United States for use both as an herb and as an ornamental plant. A very good tea can be made with any verbena that you may have left over after trying this recipe. Verbena tea and also a mixture of verbena and pekoe tea are quite popular in Spanish-speaking countries. Herbalists claim that verbena has a mild antispasmodic effect that is beneficial in minor stomach and intestinal distress.

  2 tightly grasped, large handfuls verbena leaves
  1 fifth vodka
  1 cup sugar syrup

Since verbena leaves are quite wiry and springy it is difficult to get an accurate measure using a tablespoon or cup; you have to compress them by grasping tightly. If you have a small scale, about ¾ of an ounce should do it. Let the leaves steep in vodka for a week, shaking the jar occasionally, then strain them out. Be sure to press out any fluid in the leaves, since that has a good deal of flavor. Sweeten with the sugar syrup, and your verbena cordial is ready.

WORMWOOD CORDIAL AND ABSINTHE

An enormous amount of folklore surrounds the topic of wormwood. Legends attribute all sorts of properties to genuine absinthe, which is simply a liqueur containing wormwood, and the sale of commercially made absinthe is prohibited in most countries. In truth, however, both the negative and the positive effects have been grossly exaggerated. Absinthe is not an aphrodisiac, the comments of Ernest Hemingway notwithstanding. Nor is absinthe harmful unless consumed in very large amounts. One of the toxic effects of genuine absinthe if taken in large amounts is a chalky-white appearance of the skin. An example of this can be seen in the figures drinking absinthe in the café scene in the painting of Toulouse-Lautrec *The Absinthe Drinkers*. In small amounts absinthe has beneficial effects, although not of the magnitude attributed by folklore. It has slight tonic and stimulant qualities, it does an excellent job of expelling worms and parasites from the body, this being the source of the name *wormwood*, and it tends to reduce fevers. Before modern medicine developed better substances for fever reduction, absinthe was widely used for this purpose. In the nineteenth century the French army gave each man a ration of absinthe during campaigns in North Africa, where fever was a particular problem.

Wormwood is not unique in being beneficial in small amounts and toxic in excessive and abusive use. The same is true of many commonly used substances; even something as innocuous as nutmeg can be intoxicating and produce liver damage in large amounts such as tablespoons of it. Why then was absinthe singled out for widespread prohibition? This is a rather difficult question to answer, but I believe that it was because some widely circulated scare stories and scientific proof of some of the toxic effects of very large amounts of absinthe occurred about the same time as the worldwide clamor against alcoholic beverages that actually led to their prohibition in the United States, Norway, and several other countries. Alcohol and absinthe were tarred with the same brush, so to speak, and not nearly so many people were eager for the lifting of the absinthe prohibition as for the lifting of the alcohol prohibition.

Absinthe is simply a wormwood liqueur that also contains many

Liqueurs Flavored with Herbs and Spices 67

other herbs for the purpose of masking the very bitter flavor of wormwood. A variety of herb combinations is used for this purpose. The majority of them use large amounts of anise, as do the commercially made absinthe substitutes. Some commercial substitutes for absinthe are Pernod, Abisante, Herbsaint, and Ojen. None of these, however, actually contains wormwood. Other than anise, some herbs and spices used in various absinthe recipes are angelica, cinnamon, cloves, cardamom, fennel, orange, lemon, ginger, peppermint, orris root, almond, melissa, coriander, and marjoram. Two absinthe recipes are given below, one of which is anise-flavored and one not, and one recipe is given for a simple wormwood cordial. It must be remembered that wormwood, which is available at health food stores, imparts a very bitter flavor to these drinks. Unless you enjoy bitter flavors such as quinine water in a gin and tonic or black coffee without sugar, I do not recommend that you try these drinks.

Absinthe Number 1 (Anise-flavored)

- 1 pint vodka
- 2 teaspoons crumbled wormwood
- 2 teaspoons anise seed
- ½ teaspoon fennel seed
- 4 cardamom pods
- 1 teaspoon marjoram leaves
- ½ teaspoon ground coriander
- 2 teaspoons chopped angelica root
- 1⅔ cups sugar syrup

Place the vodka in a large jar with a tightly fitting top. Add the wormwood and shake well. Let the wormwood steep for 48 hours and then strain it out. It helps to work the fennel and anise seeds, as well as the contents of the cardamom pods, in a mortar for a few minutes so that the flavors in their interiors can better blend with the alcohol. Add these and the marjoram, coriander, and angelica, shake well, and let steep in a warm but not hot place for one week. Filter the contents of the jar through some clean cotton cloth, and then add the sugar syrup. At this point your absinthe is ready, but take your first sip carefully. The other ingredients help cover the bitter taste of the wormwood, but they do not mask it completely.

Absinthe Number 2

> 1 teaspoon crumbled wormwood
> 1 cup vodka
> 2 tablespoons chopped peppermint leaves (chopped to tea-leaf size)
> 1 piece of lemon peel about ¾ inch wide and 2 inches long
> ⅓–½ cup sugar syrup

Add the wormwood to the vodka in a jar, shake well, and let steep for 48 hours. Strain out the wormwood, and add the peppermint leaves and lemon peel. Let steep for eight days, then strain through clean cotton cloth. Add ⅛ cup of the sugar syrup, and try the mixture cautiously. You may want to increase the sugar syrup to ½ cup. The aroma of this liqueur is delightful, but the spices in the preceding recipe for absinthe do a better job of masking the taste of the wormwood.

Wormwood Cordial

    1 teaspoon crumbled wormwood
    1 cup brandy
    ⅓ cup honey

Add the crumbled wormwood to the brandy, shake, and let steep for 48 hours. Strain through clean cotton cloth, and add the honey. Let stand for three weeks, and carefully uncap the jar without shaking it. The pollen and dark material in the honey will have settled to the bottom, and a clear attractive wormwood cordial can be siphoned off the top. This last step is not necessary unless a murky-looking drink bothers you.

Although I am not really enthralled with wormwood cordial, I find the product of this recipe bitter but drinkable. I once tried a recipe for wormwood cordial given in Euell Gibbons's excellent book *Stalking the Healthful Herbs*, which calls for 2 ounces of wormwood in a pint of brandy among other ingredients. I could not even drink the results, nor could any of my friends, including one who will usually drink anything with alcohol. (On one occasion I even saw him drink tequila from a bottle containing a worm, but even he could not get down wormwood cordial when made according to Gibbons's recipe.)

❖

Zebrovka

Zebrovka, also known as European buffalo grass, is used to add flavor and aroma to the finest Polish and Russian vodkas. Technically speaking, zebrovka-flavored vodka is not a liqueur or cordial because it is not sweetened, but I am including it because it is a pleasant herb-flavored drink. Simply put two blades of zebrovka in a fifth of vodka and leave them in it. In Russia, zebrovka-flavored vodka is often served cold and straight, sometimes with a little pepper added. Zebrovka may be obtained from Aphrodisia Products, Inc. (see page 38). It sells for 95 cents for ⅛ ounce, and that is all you need.

Coltea-Blend Herb Liqueur

Coltea is a mixture of herbs blended for tea and marketed by the Meadowbrook Herb Garden Company (see page 38). Sweetened with honey, it is a delicious herb tea that I enjoy very much. About two years ago I began making liqueurs with it and was gratified to find that the liqueur is even better than the tea. It has a pleasant herbal taste that is slightly bittersweet with a mild licorice-anise undertone. The list of herbs Meadowbrook puts in Coltea is extensive: sage, thyme, fennel, islandic moss, ground ivy, blackberry leaves, mullein, yarrow, cowslip, plantain, anise, licorice, hyssop, and linden flowers. The flavor can be altered to some extent by increasing or decreasing the amount of herb tea or by varying the steeping time. Of the various permutations I have tried, the one listed below is the recipe I like best.

- 6 tablespoons Coltea blend
- 1 fifth vodka
- 1 cup sugar syrup or honey

Let the herbs steep in the vodka for two weeks, then pour through a wire strainer, pressing out any liquid remaining in the herbs. Filter through cloth several times, and sweeten. Honey produces a flavor superior to sugar syrup, and the difference is worth it if you do not mind the extra step of clarifying. This is an especially enjoyable liqueur on a cold winter evening.

4

Recipes for Fruit-Flavored Cordials and Liqueurs

Fruit-flavored liqueurs and cordials are somewhat more difficult to make than herb-flavored ones, since the flavor and the sugar content of fruit vary. However, these recipes were developed with considerable testing and experimentation, so that only minor adjustment of the amount of sweetening may be necessary after your liqueur is completed. Commercial fruit liqueurs are made much like these recipes, although sometimes the remaining fruit residue is distilled and this material added to the liquid in which the fruit has steeped.

Some of the terms regarding fruit-flavored liqueurs can be a bit confusing. Although there is no longer any real distinction between the terms "cordial" and "liqueur," fruit-flavored products are more often called cordials. Another unusual feature is that the term "fruit-flavored brandy" is really a cordial or liqueur, since products so labeled are required by federal law to have a brandy base flavored with fruit, to be at least 70 proof, and to have a sugar content of at least 2½ percent. True fruit brandies or *eaux de vie* as they are called in Europe, on the other hand, are unsweetened and the distillate of naturally fermented fruit.

The products produced by these recipes are quite good. In addition to being served as drinks, they have numerous uses in the preparation of desserts and other foods. Most fruit cordials make excellent toppings on fresh or canned fruit of the same type; other suggestions may be found in Chapter 1. For a truly unusual treat, buy some of the hollow chocolates available in stores around Easter time, make a small hole in them, and with an eyedropper fill them up with your favorite fruit liqueur. Cherry is delicious in them. The hole can be sealed up by melting a little of the chocolate in the area with a heated spoon. These cordial-filled candies are made commercially in Austria and Germany, but not in the United States. Our lawmakers, concerned that children would get hold of these candies and consume so many as to become intoxicated, have prohibited their sale.

Although I think that all the recipes presented in this section make good liqueurs, my personal favorites are: apricot number 1, banana, blackberry, cherry numbers 1 and 2, currant, all of the orange ones, prune, quince, and raspberry.

APRICOT LIQUEURS

Apricot cordial and apricot-flavored brandy are good fruit-flavored liqueurs, and some versions can be made in the kitchen without difficulty. There are also a number of commercial varieties of both American and French manufacture. To my taste the French brands such as Marie Brizard and Dolfi are superior to the American. Perhaps this is because the apricots from the Loire Valley in France are considered the world's best. (This is a bit strange, since the apricot originated in northern China and is widely cultivated in the Orient.) Some health-food faddists believe that the apricot and especially its seeds contain a mysterious ingredient that will some day be acclaimed as another vitamin. Their basis for this claim is that the Hunza, a people in a remote area of the Himalayas whose main food is apricot fruit and oil from the seed, have remarkably good health and great longevity. Many Chinese, including the ancient philosopher Lao-tzu, also have believed that the apricot had extraordinary properties.

Apricot Liqueur Number 1

- ½ pound dried apricots
- 16 ounces water
- 2 teaspoons powdered sugar
- 12 ounces vodka
- 4 ounces brandy
- 1½ tablespoons sugar syrup

Boil the dried apricots in the water for several minutes, and baste them with the water while the cooking is taking place. The aim here is to get as much of the water absorbed by the dried fruit as possible. When very little water is left, let the apricots cool and put them in a large jar with the powdered sugar sprinkled over them. Add the vodka and brandy, and shake well. If the fruit is not completely covered by liquid, push it down with a spoon. If it is still not completely covered, add a little more vodka until it is. Close the jar tightly, and let steep for two weeks. Pour off the liquid, and mash the fruit in a bowl until as much as possible of the liquid is extracted from it; a cloth jelly bag is also very good for this. The liquid that is in the fruit is richer in flavor than that which is poured off, and since it consists of vodka and brandy, it is expensive, and none should be wasted. Combine the liquid poured off with that squeezed from the fruit, add the sugar syrup, and strain through dampened clean cotton or flannel cloth a few times until any remaining fruit pulp is gone. This makes an apricot liqueur that is thick and a little syrupy, but the flavor is good and robust, and it is not too sweet. Sixteen ounces of vodka can be used instead of the brandy-vodka combination called for in the recipe, but I like the flavor that a little brandy adds. Since the flavor is strong compared to most fruit cordials, it may be diluted with a mixture that is three parts vodka and one part sugar syrup. An interesting flavor variation can be obtained by adding a small pinch of cinnamon to this liqueur.

Another apricot liqueur that is considerably easier to make is given in the following recipe. Taken by itself it is quite good, but if it is compared to the results of the first recipe it suffers from the comparison.

Apricot Liqueur Number 2

> 6 rounded tablespoons of good apricot jam with a lot of fruit in it
> 1 fifth brandy or 24 ounces brandy-vodka combination
> 2 tablespoons of honey

Whip the jam and brandy well in a blender, put in a tightly closed jar, and store in a warm but not hot place for six weeks. Strain through cloth and add the honey, mixing it well. I prefer my liqueurs a little on the dry side; you may want to use a little more honey to taste.

The flavor of the recipe based on dried fruit is superior to the one using jam, since apricots retain their flavor well when dried. As fresh apricots are not available for most of the year in the area where I live, I have not developed a recipe using the fresh fruit. I have had the liqueur made by a friend living in the fruit-growing region of the Santa Clara Valley who makes it with a combination of fruit and seed. It was quite good with an almond undertone which was probably from the seed. I have also seen a recipe for a liqueur in *Larousse Gastronomique* based on just the seeds of apricots and peaches. This is definitely an alcoholic beverage that should be used in moderation, since peach seeds contain prussic acid, which is poisonous in quantity.

The apricot liqueurs made by these recipes are quite good in mixed drinks and served over chilled fruit such as melon. In mixed drinks they are good with the juice of a lemon and sweetening with soda water in a tall glass with ice.

❖

Banana Liqueur

A very pleasant liqueur flavored with fresh bananas can be made without much difficulty. It should not be confused with crème de ananas, a pineapple-flavored cordial made in France.

    1 medium-sized ripe banana
    1 fifth vodka
    1 cup sugar syrup
    ¾ teaspoon pure vanilla extract

Peel and mash the banana, and put it into a large jar. Add the vodka, making sure the banana is completely covered. Close the jar tightly and let steep for one week. At the end of the week pour the contents through a wire strainer to remove most of the banana, and then add the sugar syrup. Strain the solution through clean cotton cloth a couple of times so that the remaining small particles of banana are removed and all the cloudiness is gone. Add the vanilla, shake well, and the banana liqueur is complete.

Blackberry Cordial

Blackberry brandy is really blackberry-flavored brandy, which is a cordial or liqueur. It is a very tasty drink and has been made in American homes since colonial times, although this is no longer widely done. I have tried making it from canned berries, extracts, jams, and even blackberry pancake syrup, but all of these are so unimpressive when compared with the flavor of the cordial made from freshly picked wild fruit that I am including only that one recipe. The flavor is remarkably good and seems to contain the very essence of the fruit. The flavor resulting from fresh cultivated berries is also good, but it does not equal that from wild berries. Blackberry brandy is widely used as a folk medicine remedy for diarrhea. I do not know if there is any scientific basis for this practice, but it would at least take a person's mind off his discomfort.

> 2 cups freshly picked crushed blackberries (almost 1 quart whole berries)
> 3 cups brandy
> 1½ cups sugar syrup

Put the freshly crushed berries, including the juice, into a jar with 2 cups of the brandy. Shake well, seal tightly, and let steep a week. Then pour the mixture through a wire strainer several times, being sure to press out all the liquid, and strain well through clean cloth or a jelly bag. Add the cup of remaining brandy and the sugar syrup. The result is remarkably delicious. If you are unable to get enough blackberries, this recipe can be divided into smaller portions. I have made it with as little as ½ cup of crushed berries (1 cup of whole berries). It is, however, important to ensure that the alcohol in which the berries steep is in the correct proportion. Although I am very fond of spices, this drink is so good I consider it almost a defilement to add anything to the flavor of the fresh berries, but if you do not have my hang-up, some of the spices and spice combinations that are traditionally added to blackberry cordial are: cinnamon; clove and cinnamon; cinnamon and nutmeg; cinnamon, clove and mace; or cinnamon and coriander.

If you have to pick all the berries for this drink yourself, you will probably consider it precious, and use it only on special occasions. At least that was my attitude toward it until I hit upon

Fruit-Flavored Cordials and Liqueurs

the solution of paying some of the local children to collect the wild blackberries that grow in profusion near my Maryland home. If you can do this, you may want to consider additional uses such as in sours or as a topping on ice cream or grapefruit.

Currant Cordial or Crème de Cassis

Currant-based liqueurs, and especially crème de cassis, which is based on black currants, are very popular in France. They have never caught on in the United States, perhaps because it is illegal to grow black currants in areas of the country where there are large stands of white pine, a commercially valuable timber tree. The reason for this prohibition is that a fungus disease that attacks the tree must spend part of its life cycle on black currant shrubs. However, I was able to develop a very tasty liqueur based on sun-dried currants packed by the Sun-Maid company which are California-grown black zante currants of good quality. I have not been as successful with other varieties or with red currants, nor have my attempts with currant jelly been successful.

- 1½ cups Sun-Maid currants
- 3 cups boiling water
- 1 fifth 80-proof vodka
- ½-1 cup sugar syrup

Cook the currants in boiling water for about 5 minutes, let them cool, and discard the water. Put the currants and the vodka into a tightly closed jar, and let steep for a week or two, giving the jar a good vigorous shaking occasionally. When the steeping is completed, strain and then filter through cloth. For sweetening I prefer to use just half a cup of sugar syrup, although one cup will make the result like commercial crème de cassis, which is quite sweet.

A very good drink which the French call kir can be made with this cordial. Fill a glass with ice and add one jigger of currant cordial or crème de cassis and about 3 or 4 ounces of dry white wine. Stir a bit, and a good cocktail or apéritif-type drink results. Many French prefer it without the ice, and sometimes champagne is used in place of the white wine. Kir, pronounced to rhyme with beer, is named after a flamboyant French clergyman who reputedly discovered the drink. An underground hero in the Second World War, he was later a priest, a member of the French Communist party, and mayor of Dijon—all simultaneously!

CHERRY LIQUEURS

Cherry liqueurs and cordials are made in many countries throughout the world with a large variety of procedures and many different types of cherries. Kirsch, an *eau de vie* type of drink, is the unsweetened distillate of fermented cherries. The ones made in Switzerland and the Black Forest region of Germany are especially good. Crème de cerise is a rather sweet cherry liqueur made in France. Cherry Heering, a delicious cherry liqueur made from the small Danish black cherry, was originally homemade by Peter F. Heering and his wife, who were grocers in nineteenth-century Copenhagen. Since most of their customers were seafaring men, their liqueur and its reputation spread throughout the world. Cherry Suisse is a Swiss combination of cherry and chocolate. Maraschino, which is based on the marasca cherry and not at all like the cherries added to cocktails, is a very good liqueur. In Japan an unusual liqueur is made from cherry blossoms.

There are basically two types of cherries, sweet and sour or tart. The three recipes given below are all based on the bing cherry, a sweet cherry that is firm and large. I have also had homemade liqueurs made by friends from the Montmorency, a tart variety that is quite good. I have tried to develop a liqueur from wild cherry bark, which is the source of commercial wild cherry flavor when it is not made artificially, but these attempts have not been successful.

Cherry Liqueur Number 1

- 2 cups ripe bing cherries
- 2 tablespoons powdered sugar
- 1 pint brandy
- 6 ounces 100-proof vodka
- 1 pinch mace
- ⅓ cup sugar syrup

The cherries should be thoroughly pricked or pierced several times each, so that the interior parts of the cherry come in contact with the alcohol solution. I use a small barbecue skewer for this, but a fork or other such instrument would probably work as well. The cherries should then be put in a jar, the powdered sugar sprinkled over them, and the brandy and vodka added. If the cherries are not covered, a little more brandy should be added until they are. Close the jar well, store in a warm place, about 80 degrees, and let the mixture set for about six weeks. Pour off the liquid, and extract any additional liquid you can from the cherries. Add the mace and the sugar syrup, shake well, and filter through cloth if necessary to get any remaining fruit particles out. Although this is relatively expensive to make, it is very good and the equal of any commercial cherry liqueur (including Cherry Heering, which costs more than $8 for a 24-ounce bottle), so the economy is considerable.

Cherry Liqueur Number 2

    3 cups cherries
    1 fifth brandy
    ¼ cup sugar syrup

This recipe produces an interesting flavor with a strong taste of almonds accompanying the cherry flavor. The cherries should be cut up and the pits removed. Then take about half of the pits, more if you want a stronger taste of almond, wrap them in cloth, and smash them with a hammer. They are too tough to crush in a mortar, and if you don't wrap them in cloth they will shoot all over. Work them over thoroughly with the hammer. You will know each time a seed breaks from the loud "pop." Put the cut-up cherries and the crushed seeds in a large jar, add the brandy, and close tightly. Let steep for about three weeks, then strain off the liquid with a wire strainer and extract any additional fluid you can from the cherries by wringing them wrapped in cloth. Add the sugar syrup, shake, and filter through cloth to remove any remaining fruit particles.

Cherry Liqueur Number 3

    ⅔ cup crushed cherry stones
    1 cup vodka
    1 small piece of a clove (break a small piece off the small end)
    1 very small pinch cinnamon
    ⅓ cup sugar syrup

Fruit-Flavored Cordials and Liqueurs 81

This recipe produces an unusual flavor that is nearly the opposite of the preceding recipe in that it tastes almost like an almond liqueur with a cherry undertone. Collect the cherry pits and crush them in the manner described in preceding recipe. Put them in the jar with the vodka, clove, and cinnamon, and let steep for three weeks. Filter through clean cotton or flannel cloth and add the sugar syrup. Small quantities are called for in this recipe because it is difficult to accumulate the seeds unless you make jam from fresh cherries. I collect mine by keeping a jar in the kitchen during the season when fresh cherries are available. My children save the seeds and add them to the jar. By the end of the cherry season there is always enough for me to use this recipe.

❖

Date Cordial

Date cordial is an unusual drink that is rarely seen unless homemade. This is surprising, since it is a good-tasting drink, and in many areas either dates or the fermented sap of the date tree is used to make wine. The fruit grows on a beautiful palm tree that frequently reaches a height of 100 feet in desert areas. It is highly nutritious, and in combination with milk is said to contain almost all the essential nutrients. The date palm provides the staple food for many desert inhabitants, and it is held in great respect in these regions. Some population authorities believe that much of North Africa and the Middle East would be uninhabited if it were not for the date palm, which requires less water than any other fruit-bearing plant.

    8 ounces pitted dates (I use half a 1-pound pack of Dromedary brand)
    1 pint 90-proof vodka
    ½ cup sugar syrup

Mash and break up the dates. Put them with the vodka in a well-sealed jar for one week, giving it a shake occasionally. After a week pour off the liquid by straining the contents of the jar with a wire strainer. Press as much liquid out of the dates as possible, and then wrap them with cloth and wring out any additional liquid. Combine these liquids, add the sugar syrup, and filter it through cloth to remove any remaining fruit pulp. You may want to add a little more sugar syrup than this recipe calls for if you like sweet, crème-type cordials.

Hawaiian Punch Liqueur

An interesting liqueur, somewhat similar to the liqueurs containing passion fruit and other tropical fruits which are commercially made in Australia, can be produced with the concentrate for Hawaiian Punch. It is a little hard to find, since most stores tend to stock the punch premixed in cans, but it is also sold as a concentrate in bottles. The "Fruit Juicy-Red" variety is the one I use, since it contains passion fruit, papaya, and guava, as well as pineapple. Although it is not one of my favorite fruit liqueurs, it is good; the tropical fruit flavor is interesting; and it is relatively easy to make.

- 2 ounces Fruit Juicy-Red Hawaiian Punch Concentrate
- 10 ounces vodka or brandy
- 2 ounces sugar syrup (more to taste)

Mix the concentrate and vodka or brandy well, and then add the sugar syrup. Many people prefer a slightly sweeter drink than this recipe calls for, so you may want to add more sugar syrup to taste. This liqueur should be filtered through cloth until the particles of fruit pulp are removed. It is especially good served over cracked ice.

ORANGE LIQUEURS

Some of the most popular liqueurs and cordials are based on the flavor of citrus fruits. Grand Marnier, considered by some to be the best liqueur, is based on oranges and brandy. I do not know if it is the best (that's a matter of individual judgment anyway), but at approximately $9 for a 23-ounce bottle it is among the most expensive. Cointreau and Triple Sec are also flavored with oranges, and Curaçao is based on the green oranges of the island of Curaçao with the addition of spices such as cinnamon and clove. Forbidden Fruit is based on a variety of grapefruit and the Valencia orange. Oddly, Forbidden Fruit is one of the most popular liqueurs in France, but it is relatively unknown in the United States, although it is made by a firm in Philadelphia. Van der Hum is a tangerine-based liqueur made in South Africa, and its title is the equivalent of the expression "What's his name?" Sabra is an Israeli-made liqueur with a flavor combination of orange and chocolate.

Liqueurs with an orange flavor are quite easy to make, as can be seen from the recipes below. Recipes for lemon, lime, and grapefruit follow. In selecting fruits for my liqueurs, I generally buy them at a health food store that features organically grown fruit, or I choose ones at the supermarket that have some green in them. This indicates that they have not been mucked with so much by produce handlers. Perfectly ripe oranges picked from the tree, especially Florida oranges, frequently contain some green. To improve their appearance for market they are often gassed with ethylene to remove the green; washed with soap, water, and Borax; and then dyed and sprayed with wax.

I also usually use Valencia oranges to make my liqueurs. These are relatively easy to find, since they comprise about half the total United States orange crop and are almost always in the supermarket from March through July.

The amount of flavor and aromatic qualities of citrus fruit vary to some extent, depending on the soil where it was growing and the weather conditions during that time. Therefore even though these recipes are based on extensive trials, a good precaution in using any recipe based on fresh citrus fruit is to sample it after the steeping by taking one tablespoon of alcohol base which is flavored from the steeping and mixing it in a cup with one teaspoon of honey or sugar syrup. If you find the flavor a little too strong, dilute the mixture by adding a little more alcohol base and sweetening in the ratio of three to one. If the flavor is a little too weak, add a bit more rind and increase the steeping time. I doubt that this problem will arise, but if it does, these procedures will remedy it.

All three of these orange-flavored liqueurs are very good, although there are slight differences between them. Number 2 is easiest to make and has a flavor similar to Grand Marnier. Number 3 is best if you want a large quantity of liqueur. If you want to explore the addition of spices beyond the cinnamon and coriander called for in recipe number 2, a very light touch of clove is interesting, as is a dash of Angostura bitters.

Orange Liqueur Number 1

    3 oranges
    1 fifth brandy or vodka
    1 cup sugar syrup or honey

Remove the peel from the oranges with a very sharp knife, taking only the outer orange-colored portion of the peel, since the inner white portion contains a bitter substance that will give your liqueur an off-taste. Place the peel with the brandy or vodka in a large jar or bottle, close tightly, and shake well. Let

Fruit-Flavored Cordials and Liqueurs

it stand for three weeks, then strain out the peel and add the sugar syrup or honey. The superior flavor of liqueurs made with honey is more pronounced with the orange flavor than with many others. Shake well after sweetening, and if you have used honey, clarify by siphoning (see "clarifying," page 32).

The liqueur in the following recipe is somewhat easier to make, as you do not have to peel oranges, and the three-week steeping time is not called for.

Orange Liqueur Number 2

    1 fifth good California brandy — *KBO FRENCH BRANDY*
2½ 1½ teaspoons Wagner's Pure Orange Extract
    1 cup honey — *8oz - ½ lb solid honey — melt it first so it'll mix easier*
    ½ teaspoon glycerine
    1 very small pinch cinnamon
    1 very small pinch powdered coriander

Mix all the ingredients in a large jar or bottle, and shake well. Let the mixture stand for about a month for the cloudy pollen particles in the honey to settle out, then clarify by siphoning (see page 32). This is a very good liqueur similar in flavor to Grand Marnier at less than half the cost per ounce. If you are unable to get Wagner's extract, other orange flavors may be substituted provided they are pure and not based on artificial ingredients. Since the different brands vary in strength of flavor, a little more than 1½ teaspoons may be necessary. After mixing the ingredients, if you decide that the orange flavor should be stronger, add the additional extract slowly in ¼-teaspoon increments.

★ Filter through the Melita coffee filter & it'll be nice & clear.

A different procedure for making orange-flavored liqueur is given in the following recipe. This is an old family recipe of a friend who makes liqueurs, and it is unusual in that approximately two quarts of liqueur are produced by a single orange.

Orange Liqueur Number 3

    1 gallon-sized wide-mouth jar
    1 fifth grain alcohol, 190-proof
    1 orange (preferably from an organic food store)
    1 piece cotton string about 3 yards long
  16 to 20 ounces sugar syrup or honey, depending on taste
    1 fifth distilled or boiled and cooled water

The wide-mouth jar can be obtained from almost any restaurant or diner. They receive mayonnaise, relish, and so on in these jars and discard them regularly. Be sure to wash the jar and lid well to get rid of any odors; using an electric dishwasher or letting a Clorox solution stand in it for a few days gets rid of contaminating tastes.

Pour the bottle of grain alcohol into the clean jar. Next, make a "cradle" for the orange with the string by firmly tying several loops around the orange so that it can be suspended above the alcohol without actually touching the fluid. Let the string hang over the edge, and close the lid tightly so that the string is held in place and the alcohol cannot evaporate from the jar.

Let the jar sit in a warm but not hot place for six weeks. Although the orange does not touch the fluid, the volatile aromatic oils in the orange will blend nicely with the alcohol during this time without any work on your part. After six weeks the orange will look shriveled up and rather disgusting. Open the jar and throw the orange away. Add 16 ounces of the sugar syrup or

Fruit-Flavored Cordials and Liqueurs

honey to the bottle of distilled or boiled water, and mix thoroughly. Then combine with the alcohol-orange solution. Up to 4 more ounces of sweetening may be added to taste if you desire a sweeter liqueur. Orange-blossom honey blends particularly well in this recipe, although honey does produce a cloudy liqueur and the extra step of siphoning to clarify (see page 33) is necessary if a clear liqueur is desired. Regardless of whether you use honey or sugar syrup, however, this recipe produces a delicious liqueur of about 71.5 proof. A variation which makes it come out at approximately 90 proof is to warm the bottle of water called for in the recipe, thoroughly dissolve 16 ounces of powdered sugar in it, and use this rather than honey or sugar syrup as sweetening. But I find this a bit too strong and prefer it at the lower proof.

OTHER CITRUS FRUIT LIQUEURS

Lemons, limes, grapefruit, tangerines, and citron can all be used in making liqueurs. I have conducted considerable experimentation with the first three, and the more successful recipes are presented here. I have not made liqueurs with either tangerines or citron. However, tangerine and spices are the basis of a good South African liqueur, Van der Hum, and citron, that unusual citrus fruit grown for the sake of its peel, which is candied and used in confections and baking, is widely used in making liqueurs in southern Europe.

Lemon Cordial

> 4 lemons or 1½ teaspoons of good lemon extract
> 1 fifth vodka or brandy
> 1 cup sugar syrup or honey

The lemons must be peeled with a sharp knife so that only the yellow outer portion of the peel is used. If you accidentally get some of the white inner peel, which imparts a bitter taste, try to scrape it off. Let the peel steep in the alcohol base for two weeks, then strain it out and sweeten. A good pure lemon extract such as McCormick's can be substituted, but I prefer the taste when fresh lemon is used. For a flavor variation a small amount of ground clove may be added, but remember that clove is a powerful spice and go lightly.

Parfait Amour is a rather sweet liqueur popular with women in France. Although there are dozens of variations on the recipe, it is basically a lemon-flavored liqueur with a touch of orange and some vanilla. Other spices may also be used.

Parfait Amour

- 1 fifth brandy or 12 ounces brandy and 12 ounces vodka
- 1½ teaspoons pure lemon flavoring
- ⅛ teaspoon pure orange flavoring
- 1 piece of vanilla bean about 3 inches long
- ½ teaspoon glycerine
- 1–2 cups sugar syrup

Combine ingredients except for sugar syrup in a large jar, and shake well. Let stand for two weeks, and then remove the vanilla bean. It may be necessary to filter through cloth if the particles of vanilla bean cannot be removed by decanting. To be authentic the liqueur should contain close to two cups of sugar syrup, but I prefer to use just a cup. I suggest that you add a cup of sugar syrup, stir well, and taste. If you desire a sweeter drink, slowly add more, tasting as you go. If you wish to experiment with this drink, other spices used in some recipes are mace, clove, cinnamon, and cardamom. Vanilla is often omitted when these other spices are used.

I have tried making liqueur from limes, but a liqueur based solely on limes does not taste especially good. A lemon-lime combination, however, makes a delicious liqueur.

Lemon-Lime Liqueur

    2 lemons
    2 limes
    1 fifth vodka
    1 cup sugar syrup
    Green food coloring (optional)

Using a sharp knife, remove the outer peel from the lemons and limes, scraping off any white inner peel. Place peels in a tightly closed jar with the vodka for two weeks. Strain out the peel, and add the sugar syrup. Add coloring if you wish. The result of this recipe is very tasty.

Grapefruit Liqueur Number 1

    2 grapefruits
    1 fifth brandy
    1 cup sugar syrup

Remove the outer peel of the grapefruit with a sharp knife, and let the peel stand in the brandy for two weeks. Since grapefruits vary considerably in size and amount of aromatic oil present in the peel, it is necessary to test at the end of the steeping time before the sweetening is added. This is done by taking a tablespoon of the grapefruit-brandy solution and a teaspoon of sugar syrup and mixing them in a cup. If the amount of grapefruit flavor seems right, it is ready to sweeten. If the flavor is too weak add the peel of another grapefruit and let it stand in the brandy for another week; if the flavor is too strong, remove the peel and sweeten, and then dilute by adding a mixture of three parts brandy to one part sugar syrup.

Grapefruit Liqueur Number 2

1 grapefruit
2 Valencia oranges
1 fifth brandy
1 small pinch powdered coriander
1 small pinch powdered cinnamon
1 cup honey

This is a pleasant liqueur similar to Forbidden Fruit. Carefully remove the outer peels of the grapefruit and oranges, discarding any white inner peel. Mix the peels, brandy, coriander, and cinnamon, and marinate in a tightly closed jar for two weeks. Remove the peel, and add the honey. If you desire a clear liqueur, it must be clarified by siphoning after the pollen in the honey has settled to the bottom, as described on page 33.

A simple liqueur with a very pleasant taste may be made by steeping peel from three citrus fruits.

Three-Fruit Citrus Liqueur

   1 grapefruit
   1 orange
   1 lemon
   1 fifth vodka
   1 cup sugar syrup

Remove the outer peel only of the fruit carefully with a sharp knife. Let the peel stand in the vodka for two weeks, strain, and add the sugar syrup.

❖

Peach Liqueur

Peach liqueur is a delicious drink, and it can be made without difficulty. Since peaches are the third most important fruit crop in the United States, after apples and oranges, it is not surprising that several American firms make a peach cordial or liqueur. Southern Comfort, an American-made liqueur with a closely guarded secret formula, contains peaches and bourbon among other ingredients. This peach-flavored cordial can be used in a number of cocktail or punch recipes, including the old American favorite "fish house punch."

   9 small fresh peaches
   1 fifth 80-proof vodka
   1 cup sugar syrup

Peel the peaches and cut them into small pieces, discarding the skins and pits. Put the peaches in a large jar with the vodka, and let them marinate for a week; it helps to give the jar a good shake during this time. At the end of that time, strain the contents through a wire strainer and press out any remaining liquid from the peaches. It also helps to wring them in cloth or a jelly bag. Add the sweetening to the liquid, and strain through cloth several times to remove any particles. The resulting drink is delicious, and the liqueur is also good as a topping for ice cream or on dessert fruits, including sliced peaches.

I have seen recipes in some European liqueur books which include the peach stones or list among ingredients just the stones and not the fruit. Such recipes must make toxicologists shudder, since peach stones contain prussic acid, which is poisonous in quantity.

Pear Cordial

Pear-flavored alcoholic beverages are not especially popular in the United States although Gallo makes a pear wine in its Ripple line. (Despite the name, it is slightly effervescent and quite good.) They are more popular in Europe. Pear wine, or perry, is made in England and France. That produced in Normandy is famous among connoisseurs. Pear *eau de vie*, or true fruit brandy distilled from fermented pears, is made on a large scale in Switzerland and France, where it is usually called poire-William. The "William" refers to the fact that it is made from the Williams pear, which is like the American Bartlett. Some of the Swiss varieties of this drink have an entire pear inside the bottle. This is accomplished by placing the bottle over the pear when it is quite small and still on the tree. However, sweetened liqueur-type pear drinks are not widely made in Europe. The following recipe produces one with a mild and delicate pear flavor.

6 pear halves from a large can of Bartlett pears in
  heavy syrup
6 ounces pear juice from the can
8 ounces 100-proof vodka
3 ounces brandy

Put ingredients in a large jar and let steep three weeks. Strain off the liquid through a wire strainer, and then mash the pears and wring them in dampened cloth. It is important to extract as much fluid from them as possible; because the flavor of this drink is mild to begin with, none of that remaining in the pears should be wasted. Remove any fruit particles by straining through cloth and carefully decanting when they settle out. I find this drink sweet enough from the sugar content of the pears themselves and the heavy syrup in which they are canned, but you may wish to add a little sugar syrup if you want something a bit more sweet.

Pineapple Liqueur or Crème de Ananas

Pineapple is a fruit of the New World, cultivated by the Indians of South America before the coming of the white man. On his second voyage to America, Christopher Columbus noticed it being eaten by the inhabitants of the island of Guadeloupe. This fruit was extremely expensive in Europe, where it was grown under glass before modern transportation made it possible to import from tropical regions without spoiling. Both wine and cordials are made from pineapple, and crème de ananas is fairly popular. Although I am very fond of pineapple, especially when it is fresh and has been allowed to ripen on the plant, I am not especially fond of pineapple liqueur or wine. This recipe is included because many people who like these beverages when made commercially say that it produces very good results.

2 cups cut-up fresh pineapple
2½ cups 100-proof vodka
¼ teaspoon pure vanilla flavoring
⅔ cup sugar syrup

Marinate the cut-up pineapple in a sealed jar with the vodka and vanilla for one week. Strain through a wire strainer, and mash the remaining pineapple in the strainer to extract as much fluid and flavor as possible. After as many as possible of the fruit particles have been removed with the strainer, the drink should be sweetened and then filtered through cloth. Pour through cloth several times, gradually increasing the thickness so that all the small bits of fruit pulp are removed. This cordial must be made with a fairly high-proof vodka to prevent the fruit from spoiling while marinating, but it can afterward be diluted to taste by adding a little pineapple juice and sweetening in the proportions that please you.

Plum Cordial

Plums grow in many different varieties all over the world, and are used in a large number of alcohol beverages in many different countries. In Japan a delicious wine is made from plums, and in numerous countries *eau de vie* brandies and liqueurs are produced from plums. Slivovitz is a famous *eau de vie* type of plum brandy made in Hungary and the Balkan countries. Quetsch is a delicious plum liqueur made in Alsace. The final product exists in a variety of colors, since plums may be any of several colors from yellow to deep violet. I generally use reddish ones in my liqueurs, not because they are any better than the other varieties but because of the pretty color of the final liqueur.

Although I have not yet tried it, I hope to develop a liqueur from the wild beach plums that grow in sandy places along the Atlantic coast. These are too sour to eat raw but very good when

Fruit-Flavored Cordials and Liqueurs

cooked with sugar. The same native Cape Codders who breathe a sigh of relief when the tourists go home in September make a delicious jam from this fruit, so it certainly should make a fine liqueur.

>   7 plums, each cut into 3 or 4 pieces
>   1 fifth 100-proof vodka
>   1 cup sugar syrup

Let the cut-up plums marinate in the vodka for about a week and a half. Pour off the liquid by using a wire strainer, and then mash the plums and wring them in cloth to extract any additional fluid. The sugar syrup should then be added and the liqueur filtered through cloth to remove any fruit pieces. This is a tasty liqueur that can be served in a variety of ways. In the Alsace, plum liqueur is often served ice cold and sipped through a lump of sugar, although that sounds a bit too sweet for me. A good dessert is cooked plums over ice cream, topped with warmed plum liqueur set aflame.

Prune Cordial

Prune cordial is an excellent one. When commercially produced, it is usually called prunelle. The best is reputed to be made in Alsace. The prune is actually a dried plum. In earlier times it was a far more important item in nutrition than it is today. Before the era of modern transportation the prune was the only fruit in the diet of people in northern regions during the winter months. Prunes have a similar advantage in home liqueurmaking; they are always available in the grocery store, and one does not have to wait for them to come into season as is necessary with fresh fruit.

16 ounces (1 package) prunes
1 quart water
4 teaspoons powdered sugar
1 fifth 100-proof vodka
1 cup sugar syrup

Boil the prunes in the water for at least 5 minutes. Discard the remaining water after they have cooled. Put them in a large jar, sprinkle with powdered sugar, add the vodka, and let steep for two weeks in a warm but not hot place. Strain off the liquid. If you think you may get any additional liquid, try mashing the prunes and squeezing them, but I am not usually able to get any from prunes. Add the sweetening syrup, and filter through cloth to remove any bits or pieces of fruit. The resulting liqueur is remarkably good, and somewhat reminiscent of fine cognac in being at once smooth and potent.

Quince Liqueur

Except as jams and jellies, quince is rarely seen in the United States. It is almost never available in the produce section of supermarkets, and fresh quinces are usually found only at roadside stands in areas where they are grown or in specialty food shops. This is unfortunate because many pleasant foods and a very good liqueur called coinguarde in France can be made from quinces. The current lack of use of quinces is strange, since the fruit has been cultivated for at least four thousand years and was much used in colonial America. In fact quince seeds were one of the first items the earliest settlers requested from England. In past years quinces were eaten; the blossoms were used as a source of perfume; and the fruit was sometimes used as a hair dye. A delicious food frequently made in Spanish-speaking countries is a quince paste that is served in combination with soft cheese. Perhaps the reason it is not in as much use currently is that quince

Fruit-Flavored Cordials and Liqueurs 97

takes some preparation, which is not in vogue in this age of fast foods. Although its aroma is quite good, the fruit is a bit too tart and astringent to be eaten raw. It is quite good roasted or as a filling in pastry. Since it has a full flavor and large amounts of pectin, it is very good for making jams and jellies, and that is the source of quince for this recipe.

   8 tablespoons quince jelly or jam
   1 fifth 80-proof vodka
   Sugar syrup to taste (optional)

Any quince jelly or jam, such as house brands in the large supermarket chains, is good in this recipe, but I have got an outstandingly rich flavor from using the Sharon Valley 778 brand, a jam imported from Israel and sold in gourmet food departments. The color of the finished liqueur is also better; it is deep gold, whereas domestic quince jelly makes a pale yellow product.

Put the jam in a jar with the vodka, seal and shake it very well. Let stand for three weeks, and then filter through cloth. I find that the sugar content of the jam or jelly imparts sufficient sweetness, but you may wish to add a little sugar syrup to taste. This recipe is also quite good in smaller quantities if the amounts are reduced proportionately.

Raspberry Cordial or Crème de Framboises

Raspberries make an excellent cordial which is quite easy to prepare and used to be very popular. It seems that every cookbook, English, American, or French, if it is more than fifty years old and mentions alcohol beverages at all, has a recipe for raspberry cordial. Both *eaux de vie* and sweetened liqueur-type drinks are made commercially in Europe, and this is sometimes confusing, because either type can be called "framboise." Raspberries are not so common in American markets except as jams, perhaps because they are fragile and more perishable than strawberries. But anyway the wild raspberries have a better and more delicate flavor. Herbalists make use of the leaves as well as the berries. After seeing packets of raspberry leaves on sale in a tiny Appalachian grocery, I inquired as to their use and was told that a tea brewed from the leaves is used to treat mouth sores and diarrhea. I do not know if there is any scientific basis for this, but I have noticed that even in years when infestations of Japanese beetles are particularly bad, they do not attack the leaves of the wild raspberry bushes near my home, so I presume that the leaves do contain some kind of unusual substance. The following recipe was developed with wild raspberries, but cultivated ones could be substituted.

    1 cup ripe raspberries
    2 cups brandy
    ¾ cup sugar syrup

Put the raspberries in a jar, and add the brandy. As with most perishable fruits, it is very important that the raspberries be completely covered with brandy. If they are not, more brandy should be added. Close the jar well, and give it a strong shaking. Let it steep for one week, and strain through a wire strainer, crushing any unbroken berries to get all the juice. Add the sugar syrup, and strain through cloth. This produces a tasty cordial that is a beautiful shade of red. Many different spices can be added to raspberry cordial, but I prefer the delicate flavor of this fruit without any additions. If you wish to try additions, some of the substances typically added are: cinnamon, clove, vanilla, orris root, or orange flower petals. If you also wish to explore another method of making the cordial, M. Grieve, in her outstanding two-volume work *A Modern Herbal*, gives a good recipe based on cooking them in a double boiler to obtain the juice.

Maud Grieve's Raspberry Cordial

"Pick fine dry fruit, put it in a stone jar, and the jar into a kettle of water, or on a hot hearth, till the juice will run; strain, and to every pint add ½ lb. of sugar, give one boil and skim it; when cold, put equal quantities of juice and brandy, shake well and bottle. Some people prefer it stronger of the brandy."

(Quoted from Mrs. M. Grieve, *A Modern Herbal*, Vol. II)

STRAWBERRY CORDIALS OR FRAISES

Strawberry cordial can be made in the home by several methods. While it is good, it does not possess the richness of flavor that can be obtained with some of the other berries such as blackberries or raspberries. I am not certain of the reason for this. It may be that the substances in the fruit which provide the flavor are less soluble in an alcohol solution than are those in the other fruits, or it may be that the modern cultivated strawberry is not as flavorful as the other berries. It is true that my cordials of blackberry and raspberry have always been made with wild fruit, and my strawberry cordial has always been made with cultivated berries. Agricultural scientists state that except for the cranberry, the flavor of wild berries always surpasses that of cultivated ones. People who have tasted the wild strawberry, which is much smaller than cultivated ones, say that the flavor of the wild variety is incomparably better. In France when strawberry liqueur is made commercially it is called "fraise" if cultivated strawberries are used and "fraise de bois" if the wild variety is used. Connoisseurs consider the latter to be much superior.

I do not know how these recipes would come out if wild strawberries were substituted, but if you have access to them, I suggest that you try substituting them in the first of the two recipes.

Strawberry Cordial Number 1

    2 cups fresh strawberries
    2 tablespoons powdered sugar
    2 cups 80-proof vodka
    ¼ cup sugar syrup

Wash the berries, remove stems, and cut each berry into two or three pieces. Place them in the jar in which they are going to steep, and sprinkle the powdered sugar over them. Pour the vodka over them, close the jar tightly, and let steep for one week. After steeping, strain with a wire strainer and crush the berries to produce all the juice possible. Add the sweetening syrup and filter through cloth several times, beginning with cheesecloth if you have it, or cotton of a very coarse weave, and then going to a more dense weave or two or three thicknesses of cloth. When all the pulp has been removed the cordial is ready.

Another recipe for strawberry cordial is useful when fresh strawberries are not in season, and since it requires no steeping time, it can be made in one day. Like the preceding recipe, it produces a pleasant but not outstanding cordial, with a mild to moderate, rather than intense, flavor of strawberries.

Strawberry Cordial Number 2

    10 ounces (1 package) frozen strawberries
    6 ounces 100-proof vodka
    2 ounces sugar syrup

Fruit-Flavored Cordials and Liqueurs

Thaw the package of frozen strawberries, crush them, and pour through a wire strainer. Mix them and press with a spoon in the strainer to get as much juice as possible out of them. The ten-ounce package should yield close to 6 ounces of juice. Do not discard the remains of the berries; they are good over cereal or ice cream. Add the vodka to the juice, and pour through the strainer again, and then through cheesecloth or loosely woven cotton as in the preceding recipe. Add the sweetening syrup, and filter through cloth once more. The problem is that the strawberries have a lot of mucus-like pulp that will simply clog up the cloth or filter paper if you try to filter it finely in one step. Unlike other fruit cordials, strawberry cordial is not generally spiced, although one variation that is used occasionally has a very small amount of pure vanilla extract.

❖

Rock and Rye

Rock and rye is a traditional American cordial that has been made in the home since colonial days. Early American whiskeymakers turned out a product that was relatively crude. The art of blending was developed slowly over time, and most producers were too small-scale to afford to wait several years for their profits, as adequate aging demands. Thus most early whiskeys were harsh and raw-tasting, and consumers sought ways to make them more smooth and mellow. Some anonymous individual found that adding rock candy and fruit slices to rye whiskey made it much more palatable, and this procedure spread throughout the colonies.

- 6 ounces rock candy
- 1 slice orange
- 1 slice lemon
- 2 cups blended or rye whiskey

Put all the ingredients in a jar. There are many differences of opinion on aging. Some people start using the drink after it has stood overnight. Traditionally, new batches are not started, but more whiskey or rock candy is added to the jar as needed. Since the rock candy dissolves slowly, the cordial usually tastes different each time. The fruit slices are replaced when their appearance deteriorates. More whiskey should be added or the fruit removed if it reaches bottom and projects above the level of the liquid. For flavor variation, a little lemon juice is frequently added, and other types of fruit, especially a few cherries and/or a pineapple slice, are occasionally used.

5

Miscellaneous Liqueurs and the Use of Extracts

This chapter includes the various odds and ends of recipes that do not conveniently fit under either herb-flavored or fruit-flavored ones, and it also discusses the use of extracts, especially the famous Noirot extracts. Of the recipes in this section, my favorites are coffee, crème de cacao, orange blossom, and green tea. The crème de cacao is quite tasty, but it is not as pleasing to the eye as are some other liqueurs. The tea recipes produce an unusual taste, and the green one is remarkably good providing you follow directions on steeping time. Oversteeping produces a foul and bitter brew. Just a few of the many flower-petal liqueurs are presented here. If you wish to try developing recipes of your own with petals and blossoms, you might try some of the other flower petals used in liqueurmaking: rose geraniums, roses, violets, and marigolds. Since I was not able to get petals untreated with insecticides, I have not developed recipes for these. If you enjoy the almond-flavored liqueur, you may wish to try developing a recipe with other nuts that you like. Although I have not tried making it myself, I have had some rather good walnut-flavored liqueur made by friends.

Almond Liqueur

A number of liqueurs are made from nuts and fruit stones including walnut, apricot, and peach kernels, and almond. Of this group almond is by far the most popular. Almond cordial is made by many home liqueurmakers around the Mediterranean. Their usual procedure is to steep crushed almonds in alcohol. Some of these individuals get into difficulty, however, by using bitter rather than sweet almonds, and a few have poisoned themselves from this mistake. The bitter almond is grown mainly as a source of flavorings, while the sweet ones are usually eaten whole or used in confections, almond paste, or marzipan. The problem is that the bitter almond contains about 6 to 8 percent prussic acid by weight. If a cordial is made from these nuts, it must be used temperately indeed, because large amounts are very toxic. Since most of the almonds produced in the United States are the sweet variety, this is rarely a problem here. If you have an almond tree growing nearby and are concerned about whether it is bitter or sweet, check the blossoms when it is in bloom. The sweet almond has pink flowers, and the bitter has white. Another difference is that the nuts of the bitter almond are more irregular than the sweet. Commercial almond extracts are usually made from the bitter almond because it has more flavor, but obviously the toxic material is not included in the extract. I use commercial almond extract for this liqueur for that reason and also because it is much faster than steeping chopped almonds.

¾ teaspoon McCormick's pure almond extract
1 fifth vodka
1 cup sugar syrup

This liqueur is very easy to make. You simply mix the ingredients together, and it is ready to use. For flavor variations small pinches of mace or cinnamon may be added.

CHOCOLATE LIQUEURS OR CRÈME DE CACAO

Chocolate liqueur, or crème de cacao, is a pleasant and versatile cordial that can be used in many food and drink recipes. The chocolate flavor is derived from the cacao bean, which originated in tropical America. Although this bean was prized by the Aztecs, who even used it as a form of payment for taxes, it was the Spanish who discovered that the flavor is greatly improved by the addition of sugar and a little vanilla. Unfortunately, crème de cacao is difficult to make in the home, and I have had more trouble developing a recipe for this liqueur than I have had for any other. I am still not completely satisfied with the recipes presented here because although the flavor is quite good the appearance is somewhat murky. However, these recipes were the best that I could produce after considerable experimentation. If any reader develops a better one, I would appreciate being sent a copy (in care of the publisher). The basic difficulty is that chocolate is soluble in fats and oils but when one tries to dissolve it in water or water-alcohol solutions, an emulsion rather than a solution results. Thus there are problems not only of a murky appearance but also of the chocolate precipitating to the bottom of the bottle. I have tried using many different kinds of powdered cacao, chocolate syrup, solid baking chocolate, and the clear chocolate flavoring made by some spice companies. This last was the only one that produced a drink without a murky appearance, but the flavor was weak and insipid. I am told that commercial liqueur producers steep the cacao beans themselves in alcohol to produce the chocolate flavor. One commercial liqueur that is very good is Vandermint, which contains a large amount of chocolate in suspension, an effect most likely achieved by the use of chemical emulsifiers. Despite their murky appearance, however, the taste of the liqueurs produced by these recipes is quite good.

Crème de Cacao Number 1

> 6 tablespoons Hershey's chocolate syrup
> 1 fifth vodka
> ½ cup sugar syrup

Mix the chocolate syrup, the vodka, and the sugar solution in a large jar or bottle and shake well. Filtering through a cotton cloth helps the cloudy appearance a little. The chocolate tends to settle to the bottom of the bottle, so it should be shaken before using.

Chocolate Liqueur Number 2

> 8 tablespoons Droste's imported Dutch process cacao
> 1 fifth vodka
> 1½ cups sugar syrup
> 1 teaspoon pure vanilla extract

This liqueur has a richer taste than the first, because of the superior flavor of Dutch-processed cacao. Stir the cacao into a little vodka in a cup until it is dissolved as best you can get it. Gradually add a little more vodka, mixing as you add. Mix this cacao solution, and add the rest of the vodka, the sugar syrup, and the vanilla in a large bottle. Shake well, and shake it again several times during a two-week period, and then let it stand undisturbed for one month. Much of the chocolate will settle to the bottom, but its flavor will blend with the alcohol. After this month is over, decant the liquid, and discard the chocolate that has precipitated to the bottom. The liqueur should be shaken a little before using.

Liqueurs and the Use of Extracts

It has a chocolate flavor that is remarkably good mixed with half crème de menthe and served over ice.

❖

Coffee Liqueur

Coffee-flavored liqueurs and cordials such as Kahlúa or Tia Maria are among the most popular, but unfortunately they are also quite expensive at more than $7 for a 23-ounce bottle. A very good coffee liqueur close to these in flavor can be made in the home for about one-third the cost. The liqueur produced by this recipe can be used in any food or mixed drink (such as a Black Russian) that calls for Kahlúa.

    1 two-inch piece of vanilla bean
3¾ cups sugar
    7 tablespoons good instant coffee (6 tablespoons if freeze-dried)
    1 fifth vodka
    2 teaspoons glycerine
      Caramel coloring (optional)

Cut the vanilla bean in two or three pieces, add the sugar and 2 cups of water in a saucepan, boil for 30 minutes, and then let cool. Dissolve the instant coffee in ¼ cup of boiling water. In a large jar or half-gallon bottle mix this coffee, the cooled sugar-vanilla solution, the vodka, and the glycerine. If a darker color is desired, add some caramel coloring. Seal the jar or bottle, shake well, and let stand for two weeks. Small particles from the vanilla bean will settle to the bottom during this time, so the bottle should be moved gently when you go to use it. I have always been able to avoid the vanilla bean particles in my finished product by carefully decanting at this stage; however, filtering through a couple of thicknesses of clean cloth will get rid of any that you cannot remove by decanting.

A large number of variations are possible with this recipe. Made with vodka, the flavor is close to Kahlúa; made with rum, especially a dark one, the flavor is closer to Tia Maria. A spicy flavor can be obtained by adding a little cinnamon, clove, and orange peel. Another spice that really enhances the flavor of coffee liqueur is cardamom. Remove the pods and crush the seeds of four cardamoms per 8 ounces of coffee liqueur, and let the mixture steep for a week or two. Filter through cloth before using.

A single cardamom pod is also quite good in a cup of hot coffee. Coffee is frequently served this way in Arab countries. Botanists believe that coffee originated in either Arabia or Ethiopia, and the name comes from the Arabic *qahwah*. If you have made some other liqueurs, many of these will blend well with the coffee liqueur. A touch of apricot or mint liqueur is a nice addition, and half coffee and half chocolate gives a good mocha flavor. I usually make coffee liqueur according to the recipe given, and then pour off about 8 ounces to try one of these variations.

There are also many uses for coffee liqueur in food and drink recipes. It is especially good as a topping for vanilla ice cream, and for drinks it is good in milk over ice or diluted with either vodka or brandy over ice.

LIQUEURS MADE FROM FLOWER PETALS

Like other parts of plants, flower petals have provided a source of aroma and flavor as well as medicinal effects that have been utilized by liqueurmakers and cordialmakers for centuries. Liqueurs made from flower petals are no longer as popular on the commercial market as they have been in previous generations. Crème de Yvette, which is made from violet petals, is the only one I know of that is produced on a large scale, although many liqueurs with a number of herbs include lavender or orange-

Liqueurs and the Use of Extracts

flower petals. Home liqueurmakers, however, use flower petals on a large scale for their products, and these are usually related to the regions where particular flowers are produced in abundance. Thus in warm Mediterranean climes acacia flowers are used, and in southern France, Spain, and Italy many liqueurs are based on orange-flower petals. In Japan, cherry blossoms are often used. Other flowers used to flavor liqueurs include roses, jasmine, red clover, marigold, lavender, carnations, and lemon blossoms. Although I have not experimented as extensively with flower petals as I have with fruit, herbs, and spices, I have made interesting liqueurs from lavender, orange petals, red clover, and rose hips. Botanically speaking, the rose hip is a fruit and not a flower, since it is the part that remains after the flower withers and dies, but since roses are grown mainly for their flowers the recipe is included in that category.

The first liqueur that I tried based on flower petals was lavender. This was rather strange, because I have always had an extremely negative image of lavender, associating it with a sweet "perfumey" scent used by blue-haired old ladies. However, I was enlightened by one of those now rare old-fashioned herbalists, who told me that a tea made from dried lavender petals was an excellent sedative that mildly induced a refreshing sleep without that drugged or "loggy" feeling afterward that soporific drugs leave you with. Needless to say, I tried lavender tea sweetened with honey shortly afterward and was agreeably surprised by the taste and aroma. The scent was similar to that of commercial products scented with lavender, but the natural petals had an aroma that was far less sweet and much more delicate. The taste was agreeable with a faint bitterness. I do not know about its effectiveness as a sleep inducer (your expectations influence the results on a test like that), but in my library research I did find some information which supports that claim. All I can really report is that I feel calmer after a cup of lavender tea or a small amount of lavender liqueur, but then quietly sipping any liqueur or herb tea is relaxing for me. As you may guess, shortly after trying the lavender tea I began working at a lavender liqueur. Dried lavender petals may be obtained at many health food stores that stock herb teas, especially the See-Lect brand. Dried lavender petals may be purchased by mail order from either Aphrodisia Products or the Wide World of Herbs (see page 38 for addresses).

Lavender Liqueur

> 6 tablespoons dried lavender petals
> 1 fifth 80-proof vodka
> 1 cup sugar syrup

Steep the petals in the vodka for one week, and then filter through cloth. Also squeeze out the saturated petals so that the vodka and flavor in them is not wasted. Add the sugar syrup to sweeten, and a delicious liqueur with the aroma of lavender and a pleasant bittersweet taste results.

Many parts of the orange tree are used in liqueurmaking. The orange fruit was covered in the section on fruits, but in areas where oranges are grown petals are widely used for making home liqueurs. Commercial liqueurmakers use neroli, a substance distilled from orange petals, in many liqueurs. According to taste experts, petite grain, a substance distilled from the green twigs of orange trees, is also added to many liqueurs with secret formulas. Orange petals or blossoms, used as a symbol at weddings since ancient times, can also be used to brew a light and stimulating tea. Dried orange blossoms can be obtained from most sources of dried herbs and at a fairly low price, since oranges are cultivated on a large scale and an acre of trees produces almost a ton of blossoms. Strangely, though the aroma produced by the petals is delightful, the taste is a little mild, so that some spice must be included in it.

Orange-Blossom Liqueur

- 5 tablespoons dried orange blossoms
- 1 fifth vodka or brandy
- 1 small pinch ground cloves
- 1 small pinch ground cinnamon
- 1 cup sugar syrup

Let the orange blossoms stand in a large tightly closed jar with the vodka or brandy and spices for one week. Then strain through a wire strainer, pressing on the petals with the back of a spoon. Strain through clean cotton cloth, and mix with the sugar syrup to sweeten. This liqueur has a pleasant taste and fine aroma as it stands, but some interesting variations can be obtained by adding a few pieces of the outer peel of an orange or using orange-blossom honey to sweeten if you wish to go to the extra step of clarifying the liqueur as required when honey is used.

Do not throw out the unused orange petals after the liqueur is made, since orange-blossom tea has the same enjoyable aroma. Use one rounded teaspoon per cup and, as with the liqueur, a little clove and cinnamon when brewing the tea. Honey rather than sugar should be used for the tea, as the difference between honey and sugar is far more noticeable in the tea than in the liqueur. The brewing time for a pot of this tea is 10 minutes.

Red clover is a flower much esteemed by herbalists, and it is used for many therapeutic purposes. The blossoms are reputedly antispasmodic and are also used as an expectorant and sedative.

(These qualities belong only to the red and not white clover.) The blossoms are used for these medicinal effects a great deal in the Appalachians of the United States and also in central Europe. The U.S. Dispensatory reports that the flowers have also been used in some smoking mixtures for asthma patients. In areas where the plant is used medicinally, it is generally in a tea, but sometimes it is made into a wine or a liqueur. To me the taste is interesting and rather unlike any other that I know of, but the flavor as well as the effects seem slightly medicinal. Since many people do enjoy it, I am including a recipe, but I suggest that it be tried in a small amount with only 8 ounces of alcohol base. Gather the fresh clover blossoms when they are in full bloom, discarding any that are not in good condition, and on the same day they are gathered put them in the alcohol base to steep.

Red-Clover-Blossom Liqueur

- 1 cup freshly picked red-clover blossoms
- 1 cup 80-proof vodka
- ⅓ cup sugar syrup

Put the blossoms in a jar, and cover with vodka. Push any blossoms floating above the fluid down with a spoon, and then close the jar tightly and let steep for one week. After one week, strain through a wire strainer and press the blossoms with the back of a spoon to get all the fluid out of them. Then add the sugar syrup, stir, and filter through clean cotton cloth. Curiously, this drink has a greenish cast to it when first made, but after it ages about one month it is a dark golden color.

Rose hips are the fruit of the rose that remains after the flower withers. They become flask-shaped because they are encapsulated by the end of the stem. Old books on herbs prescribe a tea made from rose hips as a remedy for a long list of ailments which careful examination reveals are all symptoms of vitamin C deficiency. In recent times it has been demonstrated that rose hips are an excellent source of this vitamin; so without knowing it, the old herbalists were actually treating vitamin C deficiency when they prescribed this tea. Rose-hip tea has been traditionally consumed during winter months in many northern regions, such as Finland and parts of Russia. Before modern transportation made fruit available during the winter, rose hips probably helped to prevent scurvy in these areas. In addition to tea, rose hips can be used to make jam, wine, and cordials. I like their flavor by itself, but I think it is far better in combination with anise. Since the rose hips require a longer steeping time than anise seed, this liqueur must be made in two steps.

❖

Rose-Hip and Anise Liqueur

3 teaspoons anise seed
1 fifth 80-proof vodka
2 tablespoons crushed rose hips
1 cup sugar syrup

Put the anise seed in a large jar or bottle with the vodka, close tightly, shake well, and let steep for one week. Then strain through clean cloth and let the rose hips steep in the vodka for one month. I use crushed rose hips from herb suppliers. If you pick your own, discard the green stem portion and crush them until the particles are about the size of small rice grains. After the rose hips have steeped for one month, filter through cloth, and add the sugar syrup. Not only does this cordial have a delicious taste, but the color is a beautiful shade of pinkish red.

TEA-FLAVORED LIQUEURS

Coffee is far more popular than tea as a beverage in the United States. Similarly, coffee liqueur is widely consumed, but tea-flavored liqueurs are almost unknown. Tea liqueur is used in France, where it is known as crème de thé, and in Italy, where it is known as crème de recco. In Japan a delicious cordial called O Cha is made from green tea, although at some $8 for a bottle of approximately 19 ounces it is quite expensive. It is interesting to speculate on whether tea might become a national beverage in the United States if coffee were to become unavailable. In the early 1600s coffee was a very popular beverage in Britain, and the coffeehouses were the center of intellectual life. However, a fungus disease wiped out the coffee plantations in the British colonies, and the empire switched to tea. Recently this same fungus disease, for which there is yet no cure, made its appearance in Brazil. If it is not contained we could become a nation of tea drinkers.

Although there are many varieties of tea on the market, there is only one tea plant. The differences in the types of tea result from local variations in soil and climatic conditions and also from the processing method employed. Black tea gets its color from a fermentation process it is put through; green tea is not fermented before drying. For hot tea I prefer black, especially the Darjeeling and Assam varieties, but I think the green tea liqueur is superior to the black. Both are good, but the green tea liqueur is really delicious. Just as in brewing hot tea, you must not steep the leaves overlong because this releases too much tannin and a bitter taste results.

Black Tea Liqueur

>   6 teaspoons good black tea leaves
>   1 fifth vodka or brandy
>   1 cup sugar syrup

   Mix the tea leaves and the vodka in jar or bottle, close, and give it a shake. Let steep just 24 hours, and then strain through cloth and add the sugar syrup. With only a 24-hour steeping time, this is one of the fastest liqueurs to make. Many of the same flavor variations that are used in hot tea can be used in this liqueur; a bit of lemon peel is good or a bit of orange peel in combination with ground clove.

Japanese Green Tea Liqueur

>   6 teaspoons green tea leaves
>   1 fifth vodka
>   1 cup sugar syrup
>   2 or 3 drops green food coloring

   As in the previous liqueur, the tea leaves should be steeped in the vodka for only 24 hours; longer steeping times make the liqueur bitter. Shake the jar or bottle well when you put the leaves in to steep, and filter through cloth 24 hours later. Add the sugar syrup to sweeten, and you have a truly delicious liqueur at a mere fraction of the cost of the imported one. For a really distinctive touch, serve this liqueur from the small sake cups which can be purchased in stores that carry imports from Japan. One way to spend a very relaxing evening is to sit in a comfortable chair with a cordial glass or two of this liqueur and

Kakuzo Okakura's classic, *The Book of Tea*, which can easily be read in one evening. It is more than a book about tea; it presents a philosophy of life.

LIQUEURS FROM EXTRACTS

There are many commercially made flavoring extracts on the market that can also be used in home liqueurmaking. The best are those made specifically for liqueurs by T. Noirot, a firm in Nancy, France. Noirot produces more than three dozen kinds of extracts, some of which have a remarkably close similarity to commercially made liqueurs, while others are unique in their own right. Below are listed some of the Noirot extracts and the commercial liqueur which they simulate.

COMMERCIAL LIQUEUR	NOIROT EQUIVALENT
Galliano	Yellow Genepy
Benedictine	Reverendine
Green Chartreuse	Green Convent
Yellow Chartreuse	Yellow Convent
Strega	Stress
Curaçao	Orange Red Curaçao
Drambuie	Honey Smoke
Goldwasser	Dantzick
Tia Maria	Moka

To make these Noirot liqueurs, simply add one cup of sugar syrup or honey and the small bottle of extract to a one-quart bottle, then fill with vodka or brandy, and shake. As in the other recipes in this book, the sugar syrup is made by boiling one cup of sugar in a half-cup of water and letting cool. If you substitute honey, use one cup, and if you want a clear liqueur the pollen in the honey must be precipitated out by letting the mixture stand a while and then siphoning to clarify it. Most liqueurs made this way taste as good as their commercial equivalents. To my taste the only exception is reverendine; to me, genuine Benedictine has a superior flavor.

Liqueurs and the Use of Extracts

These Noirot extracts have a number of advantages. A bottle of extract costs slightly more than $1, which with vodka and sweetening brings the cost of finished liqueur to approximately $6 per quart. Since many commercial liqueurs cost $9 for a 23-ounce bottle, with Noirot extracts your cost per ounce of liqueur is half what it is commercially. Other advantages of the Noirot extracts are that their sweetness or dryness can be adjusted to taste, and that Noirot uses pure ingredients which are listed on the label, so that you know what you are consuming. This increases my peace of mind while sipping a liqueur, because some commercial producers have been accused of using less than pure ingredients. From seeing the ingredients listed I also have got many ideas for my own recipes. Noirot extracts can be purchased at many establishments that stock winemaking and beermaking supplies, especially in the Wine Supply West stores which have several dozen outlets in various cities around the country. They can also be purchased by mail order from the following firms:

Wine Supply West, Inc.
4324 Geary St.
San Francisco, California 94118

Wine-Craft
3707 Valley Hill Drive
Randallstown, Maryland 21133

The Purple Foot
3171 South 92d St.
Milwaukee, Wisconsin 53227

Wine Makers Haven
105 N. York Road
Hatboro, Pennsylvania 19040

Another manufacturer of extracts for making cordials and liqueurs is Spice Club Foods, Inc. They manufacture a number of extracts, including crème de menthe, crème de cacao, kümmel, and several fruit flavors such as apricot, peach, and blackberry.

These flavors are the easiest of all to use because they are already sweetened and you simply mix the contents of their bottles with an equal amount of 100-proof vodka. However, this has drawbacks. The alcohol level of the final liqueur is low, since diluting 100-proof vodka with an equal volume of nonalcoholic fluid results in a product which is only 50 proof, hence weaker than most liqueurs. Also, the fact that these liqueurs are already sweetened prevents one from substituting honey and/or from reducing the amount of sweetening if a drier liqueur is preferred.

In addition to these extracts expressly produced for liqueur-making there are a number of food flavorings, extracts, and concentrates on the market that can be used to make very pleasing cordials and liqueurs. If you wish to experiment with these, it is best to use those products that have natural rather than artificial flavors; most artificial substitutes do not compare with the natural product in flavor. In crème de menthe, for example, artificial peppermint spirit or oil of peppermint makes a drink that is remarkably less flavorful than drinks made by steeping peppermint leaves in vodka or those produced from natural extracts of peppermint leaves.

It is also wise to use small amounts when experimenting with extracts to produce liqueurs. One cup, or eight ounces, of vodka and one-third cup of sugar syrup is a good amount to start with, and when the drink is perfected simply multiply the amount of ingredients by three for a final recipe using a fifth of alcohol base. Add the flavoring in very small amounts too. One-eighth teaspoon is good to start with, and proceed slowly. If your flavor is too weak, it is a simple matter to correct it by adding more of the flavoring source, but a drink in which the flavoring is too strong is more problematic. This can sometimes be corrected by simply serving it over shaved ice or by diluting it with more sugar syrup–vodka solution. But if it is much too strong in flavor, it frequently cannot be corrected and has to be discarded.

Appendix

Tables of Weights, Measures, and Metric Conversions

Any book of recipes ought to contain tables for the ease of users who wish to produce a different final quantity than that of the recipe. In addition, many of the better books on liqueurmaking are produced in Europe; and there, as in most of the world, the metric system of measures is used. The system of measures generally used in the United States is sometimes called the English system, because it originated in England. It is a rather illogical system, and even when the English used it, their measures were not consistent with ours. The size of the United States pint, gallon, tablespoon, and other units differed from the British ones. England, like most other countries, has now gone metric. A table of metric conversions is presented here for people in metric areas who use this book and for Americans who wish to consult other sources. The United States will probably convert to the metric system officially within the next decade. The U.S. National Bureau of Standards reports that the country is slowly going metric on its own, but in a rather uncoordinated way. American scientists have long used the metric system; the military is now using it extensively; and food packagers have begun listing quantities in both systems. The metric system is easy to use because all units within a given dimension such as weight are related to each other by powers of ten. The user does not have to memorize arbitrary units;

one merely shifts a decimal point from one unit to another to make conversions within the system. In addition, the metric system has a standard set of prefixes to relate the various units, which are:

    kilo = 1,000 times the basic unit
    deci = one-tenth the basic unit
    centi = one-hundredth the basic unit
    milli = one-thousandth the basic unit

The metric conversions in the tables below are rounded off. For example, a pound is listed in the table as 454 grams; actually it equals 453.5924 grams.

There are other simple ways to make conversions besides these tables. Pharmacists and chemists sometimes use graduated beakers scaled with notations in both systems, and these can be obtained from most chemical-supply houses. If you have a small scale, such as a postage scale or one from a chemistry set, a handy standard is a nickel coin because it weighs 5 grams. Thus, if your recipe calls for 10 grams, weigh two nickels and note where the pointer stops on the scale, and then measure out your ingredient until the needle stops at the same place. Another handy but less accurate equivalent is that most ground spices, such as cinnamon and coriander, usually weigh 2 or 2½ grams per teaspoon.

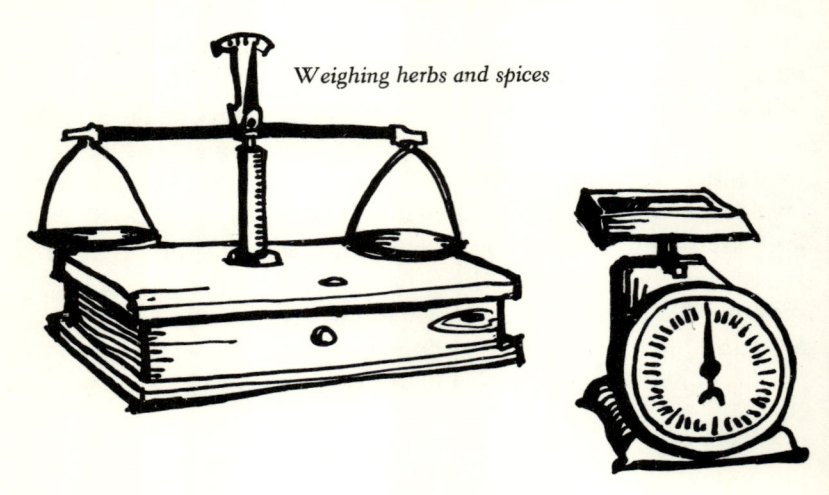

Weighing herbs and spices

Appendix 121

U.S. LIQUID OR FLUID MEASURES

1 teaspoon = ⅓ tablespoon
1 tablespoon = 3 teaspoons
1 tablespoon = ½ ounce
2 tablespoons = 1 ounce
5⅓ tablespoons = ⅓ cup
8 ounces = 1 cup
16 tablespoons = 1 cup
1 cup = ½ pint
2 cups = 1 pint
16 ounces = 1 pint
2 pints = 1 quart
32 ounces = 1 quart
4 quarts = 1 gallon
25.6 ounces = ⅕ gallon or ⅘ quart (popularly known as "fifth")
5 fifths = 1 gallon
1 barrel (liquid) = 31.5 gallons (for oil 42.5 gallons)
1 jigger or "shot" = 1½ ounces

U.S. MEASURES BY WEIGHT OR AVOIRDUPOIS AND DRY MEASURE

It should be noted that the pints and quarts in the table of dry measures are used for dealing in fresh fruits and vegetables, and they are not equal to the pints and quarts used in liquid measures. The dry measures are at least 15 percent larger.

16 drams = 1 ounce (avoirdupois)
16 ounces = 1 pound
2 pints = 1 quart
8 quarts = 1 peck
4 pecks = 1 bushel

CONVERSIONS FOR USING METRIC RECIPES IN THE UNITED STATES

Liquid and Volume Measures

1 milliliter (ml.) = ⅕ teaspoon
100 milliliters = 3.4 ounces
½ liter = 8.5 ounces
¼ liter (250 ml.) = 16.9 ounces
¾ liter = 25.3 ounces (approximately same as U.S. "fifth")
1 liter = 33.8 ounces, or 1 quart and 1.8 ounces

Weight Measures

1 gram = 1/30 ounce (avoirdupois)
100 grams = 3.5 ounces
¼ kilogram = 8.82 ounces
½ kilogram = 17.6 ounces
1 kilogram = 2.3 pounds, or 2 pounds and 3.3 ounces

CONVERSION FOR USING AMERICAN RECIPES IN A METRIC COUNTRY

Liquid and Volume Measures

1 teaspoon = 5 milliliters
1 tablespoon = 15 milliliters
1 ounce = 29.5 milliliters
1 cup (8 ounces) = 237 milliliters
1 pint (16 ounces) = 473 milliliters
⅕ gallon or "fifth" = ¾ liter
1 quart = .946 liter
½ gallon = 1.9 liters
1 gallon = 3.78 liters

Appendix

Weight Measures

> 1 ounce (avoirdupois) = 28.35 grams
> ¼ pound = 113.4 grams
> ½ pound = 226.8 grams
> 1 pound = 454 grams
> 5 pounds = 2.27 kilograms

Glossary of Cordials, Liqueurs, and Related Terms

Abricotine: a French apricot liqueur made from the small apricot that grows in Île de France.

Absinthe: an herb-flavored liqueur containing wormwood. Most versions have large amounts of anise to partially mask the bitter taste of the wormwood. Absinthe is now banned in most countries because of supposed toxic properties. A number of absinthe substitutes made without wormwood are on the market: for example, Pernod, Abisante, Herbsainte, Oxygene, Abson, and Mistra.

Advocaat: a cordial made in Holland of egg yolk, sugar, and brandy. It is a creamy emulsion similar to eggnog.

Aiguebelle: a French liqueur reputed to be flavored with more than fifty herbs.

Alkermes: a liqueur, made in Mediterranean countries, having a brandy base and flavored with orange flowers, cinnamon, and cloves.

Allasch: a type of kümmel originally made in Latvia. It is very sweet and contains almond and anise flavors in addition to caraway.

Amer Picon: a bitter French cordial flavored with oranges, quinine, and spices. It is usually served in mixed drinks rather than straight.

Anesone: an anise-flavored cordial, like anisette but sweeter and with a higher alcohol content.

Angelica: a European herb used as a flavor in many liqueurs. There is also a liqueur made in Basque country by the name; it is flavored with angelica and other herbs from the Pyrenees.

Anis del Mono: an anise-flavored liqueur, the only one I know that is fairly dry, made in Spain.

Anisette: a sweet liqueur flavored with anise seed and sometimes other ingredients such as fennel, coriander, or almond.

Apricot Liqueur: a tasty apricot-flavored liqueur made in most countries where apricots are grown (the French is reputed to be the best). If the apricot kernels are included in the process they add an almond undertone to the flavor.

Apry: a good apricot liqueur made in France by Marie Brizard.

Aquavit or Akvavit: an unsweetened liquor flavored with caraway seeds, made in Scandinavian countries. It is usually served cold and straight with appetizers before meals.

Arak: a licorice-flavored resinous liqueur made in Turkey and the eastern Mediterranean area, not to be confused with Arrack or Batavia Arak.

Armagnac: a brandy made in southwestern France, considered by many connoisseurs second only to cognac. Its unique flavor comes in part from its being aged in casks made of the black oaks of Gascony.

Arrack or Batavia Arak: a pungent liquor made in southeast Asia, especially Java, from distilled fermentations of rice and palm wine. It is frequently used as an ingredient in a punch, popular in the Netherlands and Scandinavia, called Swedish Punsch or Caloric Punsch.

Aurum: a dry Italian liqueur flavored with oranges and herbs gathered in the Abruzzi mountains.

Balsam: a banana-flavored liqueur made in the West Indies.

Banana Liqueur: a banana liqueur, usually called crème de bananes.

B and B, or Benedictine and Brandy: a drier liqueur than Benedictine.

Benedictine: an excellent herb-flavored liqueur made in France. Although the letters D.O.M., for *Deo Optimo Maximo,* or "To God, most good, most great," are on the label, this liqueur is made by a commercial firm and monks have not made it since the French Revolution. It contains more than fifty herbs and, according to some, has medicinal value, but the actual formula is a closely guarded secret supposedly known only to three people. There have been many attempts to duplicate this both on a commercial scale and in the home, but none has been able to reproduce the same flavor.

Bitters: various flavoring agents made by steeping herbs and other botanicals in alcohol. A dash or two is used to flavor many drinks and cordials.

Blackberry Cordial and Blackberry-Flavored Brandy: these are blackberry-flavored liqueurs. They are reputed in folk medicine to have an antidiarrheic effect.

Black-Currant Liqueur: also known as crème de cassis, this is an excellent cordial with a fairly low alcohol content. It is usually diluted with dry white wine in France to make an aperitif called kir.

Brazilia: a coffee-flavored liqueur, which as the name suggests is made in Brazil.

Bronte: a liqueur, produced in Yorkshire, England, having a brandy base with herb flavoring, and sweetened with honey.

Cacao mit Nuss: a liqueur made in Germany with chocolate and hazelnuts.

Calisay: a bitter Spanish liqueur flavored with cinchona bark, which contains quinine and other botanicals.

Calvados: a brandy distilled from fermented apple juice in Normandy. Legends say this drink was developed by Norsemen who settled there. In the U.S. a similar drink called applejack is made in New Jersey.

Carlsberg: an herb-flavored German liqueur that contains mineral water and is said to have medicinal value.

Cayo Verde: a lime-flavored liqueur produced in the U.S. from key limes, which are smaller and more flavorful than the Persian limes.

Centerbe: an Italian liqueur flavored, as the name suggests, with more than one hundred different types of herbs.

Cerasella: a cherry liqueur made in Italy.

Channelle: a spicy liqueur which contains cinnamon as well as other spices.

Chartreuse: this term refers to two liqueurs made by the Carthusian monks in France. The green is more expensive and is said to contain more than 230 botanicals, although the actual formula is secret. It is 110 proof, while the yellow is 86 proof and contains fewer varieties of herbs. A white chartreuse was once also produced, but it is no longer made. Around the turn of the century the Carthusians were expelled from France but continued to produce these liqueurs from Tarragona in Spain; they were allowed back into France about forty years later. During their exile the French government was involved in an attempt to duplicate and market the liqueurs at the original site, but the products were so inferior that they became a source of comedy.

Cherry Blossom: a Japanese liqueur, made by the Suntory Company, which has the delicate aroma of cherry blossoms.

Cherry Cordials and Liqueurs: many different cherry liqueurs are made in France, Germany, Denmark, Switzerland, Italy, America, England, Holland, and Yugoslavia. Most of them are quite good. There are large differences in flavor among them because of differences in both the process and the type of cherry used.

Cherry Heering: a very good but expensive liqueur produced from the distinctively flavored small Danish black cherry. It was originally a homemade liqueur produced by Peter Heering, a grocer in nineteenth-century Copenhagen.

Cherry Marnier: a high-quality cherry liqueur produced in France.

Cherry Suisse: a Swiss liqueur that combines the flavors of chocolate and cherry.

Claarava: an herb and honey liqueur produced in Scotland.

Claristine: an herb-flavored liqueur with a slight resemblance to Benedictine, produced by the Clarist nuns in France.

Cocuy: a brandy or *eau de vie* distilled from sisal roots in Venezuela.

Coffee Liqueurs: there are numerous coffee-flavored liqueurs on the market produced in many areas where the coffee bean is grown, including Brazil, West Africa, Hawaii, Jamaica, and Mexico.

Coinguarde: A quince-flavored liqueur produced in France.

Cointreau: a brand of Triple Sec or liqueur made from the green oranges of Curaçao with brandy for an alcohol base.

Cordial Medoc: a French cordial containing orange Curaçao, other flavorings, cognac, and Medoc claret.

Crème: a large class of liqueurs having a creamy consistency due to a high sugar content, and therefore very sweet.

Crème de Ananas: a liqueur containing pineapple, brandy, and vanilla.

Crème de Banana or Bananes: a yellow liqueur flavored with banana and fairly low in alcohol content, usually about 46 proof.

Crème de Cacao: a liqueur with a chocolate taste flavored with cacao beans and vanilla. The word Chouao on the label indicates that the beans were grown in the Chouao region of Venezuela, which is considered the best.

Crème de Café: a coffee-flavored liqueur.

Crème de Cassis: a black-currant liqueur, of which the best is produced in France. The alcohol content is rarely above 50 proof.

Crème de Celeri: a liqueur flavored with celery seed. Other flavors such as caraway, anise seed, and fennel may also be present.

Crème de Cerise: a sweet cherry liqueur.

Crème de Cumin: a type of kümmel produced in France. Some sugar

Glossary

is usually crystallized in the bottom of the bottle in a pleasing form.

Crème de Fraises: strawberry cordial.

Crème de Framboise: raspberry cordial.

Crème de Menthe: a peppermint cordial that is probably the most popular of all liqueurs and cordials. It is usually either clear or green-colored, although other colors are sometimes used. Occasionally other flavors, such as cinnamon, ginger, orris root, or sage, are added.

Crème de Moka: a liqueur made with coffee beans and brandy.

Crème de Noyau: an almond-flavored liqueur made from peach and apricot kernels.

Crème de Recco: a liqueur containing tea leaves, brandy, and sugar.

Crème de Roses: a liqueur flavored with rose petals. Sometimes rose hips are included with the petals, but more commonly these are used to make a separate liqueur.

Crème de Thé: this liqueur, made in France, is quite similar to the Italian Crème de Recco.

Crème de Vanille or Vanilla: a sweetened infusion of vanilla beans in an alcohol base.

Crème de Violets: a liqueur flavored with violet petals.

Crème de Yvette: a violet cordial made in Philadelphia by Jacquin Company.

Curaçao: a cordial originally made in Amsterdam but now produced in many countries from the peel of the green oranges of Curaçao. It also contains spices such as cinnamon and cloves.

Curanta y Tres: a gold-colored cordial made in Spain and, as the name suggests, containing 43 different herbs.

Damiana: a liqueur produced in Mexico and flavored with damiana leaves which are believed by many to have an aphrodisiac effect. A commercial version is imported into the United States by the Paddington Corporation.

Danzigwasser: a spicy liqueur similar to Goldwasser, originally produced in Danzig. It usually contains orange or lemon peel among its flavorings, and flecks of gold leaf are frequently added for the medicinal effect attributed to gold in European folk medicine.

Delecta: an herb-flavored liqueur somewhat similar in flavor to Benedictine but not as good.

Dewmiel: a British liqueur with a Scotch whiskey base.

Drambuie: an excellent liqueur produced in Scotland containing Scotch whiskey, heather honey, and a secret blend of Highland herbs, one of which is angelica. Legend has it that the recipe was given to the MacKinnon family as a reward by Prince Charles Edward Stuart

(Bonnie Prince Charlie) for sheltering him after his defeat in 1746. If that is the case why did the MacKinnon family not market this liqueur commercially until 1892?

Eau de Vie: a generic term for an unsweetened alcoholic beverage produced by fermenting a substance, usually fruit, and distilling it. In the United States these are sometimes called true fruit brandies. Kirsch, which is a brandy made from fermented cherries, is a good example. Switzerland produces *eaux de vie* of very high quality.

Elixir d'Anvers: a bittersweet liqueur produced in Belgium.

Elixir de Bacadi: a Cuban liqueur with a rum base.

Elixir de China: a clear sweet liqueur produced in Italy with Chinese anise.

Eltaler: yellow and green herb-flavored liqueurs produced by monks in Germany.

Enzian: a liqueur containing gentian and other herbs. It is made in Germany, where it is considered a good home remedy for stomach pains.

Escarchado: a liqueur, produced in Portugal, having an anise flavor. It is sweet and usually contains sugar crystals in the bottom of the bottle.

Espresso: a liqueur flavored with espresso coffee.

Falernum: a lime and almond flavoring produced in the Barbados of the West Indies. The alcohol content is low, and it is used to sweeten and flavor drinks.

Fiore d'Alpe or Flora Alpina: a liqueur flavored with edelweiss and other Alpine herbs. There is a twig in the bottle on which sugar crystallizes. This is a very smooth and pleasant liqueur.

Fleur de Mocha: a coffee-flavored cordial.

Forbidden Fruit: a liqueur made by the Jacquin Company in Philadelphia. The alcohol base is brandy, and the flavoring is from the shaddock, a type of grapefruit, and Valencia oranges.

Fraise: This term can refer to either an unsweetened strawberry *eau de vie* or to a sweet strawberry liqueur, so the label must be read carefully. When the term *fraisette* is used it is a sweet liqueur.

Framboise: this term applies to either an unsweetened *eau de vie* or to a sweet liqueur, in this case raspberry. Labels can be confusing, so they must be carefully checked; the term "raspberry-flavored brandy" actually means a sweetened liqueur. One way to tell is that *eau de vie* drinks made from berries are usually about 90 proof whereas the sweetened berry liqueurs are generally about 70 proof.

Glossary

Galliano: a very popular Italian liqueur flavored with herbs and spices. It is named after Major Giuseppe Galliano, a war hero in the Italian-Abyssinian conflict.

Gallweys Irish Coffee Liqueur: a coffee liqueur with an Irish whiskey base, flavored with herbs and sweetened with honey.

Geneva Gin: an unsweetened juniper-flavored liqueur. The name comes from *genièvre*, the French word for juniper.

Gilka: a kümmel, probably the best one, made in Germany.

Ginger-flavored Brandy: a liqueur made by infusing ginger in brandy. It is often sweetened, and sometimes pepper is added to make it more pungent.

Glayva: an herb- and spice-flavored liqueur made in Scotland.

Glen Mist: a liqueur made in Scotland with a Scotch whiskey base, sweetened with honey. It is less sweet than Drambuie or Glayva.

Goldwasser: a cordial made with spices and usually either lemon or orange peel. It contains tiny flecks of gold leaf, which were believed to give it medicinal value.

Gorny Doubnyak: a bitter Russian liqueur flavored with herbs, ginger, and acorns.

Grand Marnier: a good but rather expensive orange-flavored French liqueur. A fine cognac is used as the alcohol base.

Grenadine: a sweet flavoring syrup that contains no alcohol, made from pomegranates.

Guignolet: a French cherry liqueur.

Herbsaint: a liqueur used as an absinthe substitute, but containing no wormwood, produced in New Orleans.

Irish Mist: a delicate liqueur containing herbs and an Irish whiskey base, and sweetened with heather honey. It is similar to Drambuie in some ways, but it is slightly less sweet and does not have the smoky taste of Drambuie.

Izarra: a liqueur with a base of Armagnac brandy and flavored with herbs gathered in the Pyrenees.

Jägermeister: a red liqueur produced in Germany. The name means "master hunter."

Kahlúa: an excellent coffee-flavored liqueur made in Mexico.

Karpi: a Finnish liqueur made from cranberries and other fruit.

Kirsch or Kirschwasser: a true fruit brandy, or *eau de vie*, which is the unsweetened distillate of fermented cherries. The best varieties are reputed to be those made in Switzerland and the Black Forest region of Germany.

Kola Liqueur: a liqueur flavored with kola nuts, citrus peel, vanilla, and sometimes tonka beans.

Kona: a coffee liqueur made from the rich-flavored kona coffee bean.

Kümmel: a liqueur, popular in northern Europe, flavored with caraway seeds, cumin, and frequently other flavorings such as fennel. At one time the best kümmel was reputed to be made in Latvia, but now most connoisseurs consider Gilka, which is made in Germany, the best.

La Senacole: an aromatic herb-flavored liqueur made in France by Cistercian monks.

La Tintaine: a French liqueur flavored with fennel and anise, and served in a tree-shaped bottle.

Lindesfarne: an English liqueur having a whiskey base and sweetened with honey.

Liqueur des Moines: an herbal French liqueur with a cognac base.

Liqueur d'Or: a liqueur similar to Goldwasser; made in France.

Liqueur de Sapin: a liqueur flavored with herbs and spices, made in the Jura Mountains.

Lochan Ora: a recent liqueur developed in Scotland, made with an alcohol base of Chivas Regal Scotch whiskey, one of the finest whiskeys made.

Luana: a coffee-flavored liqueur.

Luxardo: a delicious Italian liqueur made with marasca or maraschino cherries. (This is a variety of cherry grown in Dalmatia and is not the type used in cocktails.)

Mandarine: a liqueur made from mandarin oranges with brandy for an alcohol base.

Maraschino: a liqueur made from the marasca cherries of Dalmatia, an area of Yugoslavia.

Marmot: a chocolate liqueur, made in Switzerland, that contains many solid bits or nibs of chocolate in the bottle.

Masticha or Mastic: liqueurs made in Greece and Cyprus from the sap of trees and anise flavoring. They are not held in high regard by connoisseurs.

Mazarine: an herbal liqueur made according to a secret formula by the monks at the Abbey of Montbenoit in Argentina.

Medoc: this term can refer to either a claret wine or a cordial that contains claret, Curaçao orange flavoring, brandy, and other ingredients.

Melisse: this term can refer to the herb melissa, and was also the name given to a white variety of Chartreuse now no longer made.

Glossary

Mille Fior d'Alpi: a liqueur made from Alpine plants. There is a miniature tree in the bottom of the bottle around which sugar crystallizes to produce a very attractive effect.

Mirabelle: a plum brandy or *eau de vie* produced in the Alsace.

Mobana: a crème-type liqueur, flavored with bananas, made in the Bahamas at Freeport.

Monastique: a commercial liqueur similar to Benedictine in that a brandy base and herb flavorings are used, but not as good as Benedictine.

Monte Aguila: a liqueur, produced in Jamaica, flavored with allspice or pimiento.

O Cha: a very tasty, rather expensive Japanese liqueur flavored with green tea.

Ojen: an anise-flavored liqueur with a high alcohol content, made in Spain.

Okolehao: this term refers to two Hawaiian liqueurs having an alcohol base made from distilled fermentations of sugar cane and rice. The white variety is flavored with coconut juice, and the dark is flavored with the root of the ti, a very decorative plant used for many purposes by the natives of the islands.

Orange Curaçao: liqueurs made with flavors from the peel of the green variety of orange grown on the island of Curaçao. Spices such as clove and cinnamon are frequently added.

Orgeat: a sweet almond-flavored syrup that also contains orange-flower petals. Used as flavoring in many drinks.

Ouzo: a liqueur made in Greece with anise flavorings. It is clear when straight but has the curious property of turning milky white when water is added. This process occurs because oils present in it are dissolved if the alcohol content is high enough, but they cannot remain dissolved if it is diluted.

Parfait Amour: a rather sweet liqueur made in many different variations in France. Some varieties are flavored with flower petals, but most are flavored with lemon peel and vanilla. Occasionally other spices are present.

Passion Fruit: a tropical fruit used to make a nonalcoholic flavoring syrup in the United States and a liqueur in Australia.

Pastis: a French term for anise-flavored liqueurs made in the vicinity of Marseilles.

Peach-flavored Brandy: this is actually a cordial, since it is sweetened. It is made by several American manufacturers.

Peach Liqueur: A liqueur sweeter and with a lower alcohol content than peach-flavored brandy.

Peppermint Schnapps: a cordial similar to crème de menthe but considerably less sweet.

Pernod: an anise-flavored cordial frequently used as an absinthe substitute since absinthe was banned. Pernod does not contain wormwood.

Perry: Fermented pear juice, somewhat like cider.

Pisco: a brandy or *eau de vie* of high quality made in Peru from muscat grapes.

Poire-William: a pear *eau de vie*, since it is the unsweetened distillate of fermented pears. In Switzerland it frequently contains a whole pear in the bottle (the bottle is placed over the pear when it is beginning to grow on the tree). The Williams pear is the European version of the Bartlett.

Prunelle: a French liqueur made with plums and prunes.

Quetsch: a clear *eau de vie* or true fruit brandy that is the unsweetened distillate of fermented plums.

Quince-flavored Brandy: a cordial made by steeping quince in brandy with sugar added. Various spices may also be added.

Raspail: a French herb-flavored liqueur with a slight resemblance to Benedictine. It is named after François Raspail, who developed it as a medicine (he may have succeeded in a small way in that it is popular as a home remedy for digestive disorders in France). Angelica is one of the herbs present.

Ratafia: a term used for cordials and liqueurs, especially those made by steeping fruit and herbs in alcohol. The term comes from a period in European history when cordials were invariably served on the occasions of ratifying treaties and pacts.

Reishu: a Japanese liqueur made from melons.

Rock and Rye: a traditional American liqueur made by steeping fruit slices, especially lemon or orange, with rock candy in rye whiskey.

Rosolio: a liqueur made from rose petals. It is not as sweet as crème de roses.

Rumona: a liqueur made in Jamaica, with an alcohol base of fine Jamaican rum and flavored with tonka beans.

St. Hallvard: an aromatic herbal liqueur made in Norway.

Sambuco: a clear liqueur flavored with licorice and herbs and made in Italy.

Glossary

Sève: a French herbal liqueur.

Slivovitz: an unsweetened *eau de vie* made from plums. Highly regarded varieties are made in Hungary, Rumania, and Israel.

Sloe Gin: a cordial rather than a gin, made from sloe berries which are the fruit of the blackthorn bush. The wild blackthorn of Devon and Cornwall is reputed to produce the best sloe gin.

Southern Comfort: a liqueur produced in the United States at 100 proof (somewhat higher than most). Although the formula is secret, two of the ingredients are bourbon and peaches.

Stonedörfer: a dark and rather bitter herbal liqueur made in Germany.

Strega: an excellent liqueur, considered by some the best of those made in Italy, flavored with a large number of herbs and spices. It has a very old and secret formula. According to legend, it was originally a love potion developed by witches.

Swedish Punsch: a liqueur, made in Scandinavia, flavored with herbs, spices, tea, and lemon. The base is Batavia Arak, an alcohol distilled from palm wine and fermented rice in the East Indies. This drink is also called Arrack Punsch or Caloric Punsch, because it gives off heat.

Tapio: a liqueur, made in Finland, flavored with herbs and juniper.

Tia Maria: a very good coffee-flavored liqueur made in Jamaica. The alcohol base is rum.

Tiddy: a light-brown liqueur sweetened with honey, made in Canada.

Trappistine: an herb-flavored liqueur made by monks in France.

Tres Castillos: an anise-flavored liqueur, sweetened with rock candy, made in Puerto Rico.

Triple Sec: this liqueur is similar to Curaçao in that it is flavored with the peel of Curaçao oranges, but it is less sweet than Curaçao. The best-known brand of Triple Sec is Cointreau.

Van der Hum: a tangerine- and herb-flavored liqueur produced in South Africa, where the expression "Van der Hum" means "What's his name?"

Vandermint: a delicious chocolate and mint liqueur produced in Holland. It is a creamy drink with a large amount of chocolate suspended in an emulsion.

Verveine du Verlay: there are actually two liqueurs, a green and a yellow, by this name. Both are herb-flavored and somewhat bitter. They are made in southwestern France.

Vieille Cure: a French liqueur made with a secret formula and said to be flavored with more than fifty different kinds of herbs. It has a brown color and is somewhat like Benedictine in flavor.

Wishiowka: a cherry liqueur similar to Wishniak but made in Russia and Czechoslovakia.

Wishniak: a cherry liqueur made in Poland.

Zubrovka: an unsweetened vodka flavored with zebrovka (European buffalo grass), which gives it a pleasant aroma and a slightly bitter taste. The zebrovka is usually left in the bottle.

Bibliography

Bennett, H. *The Chemical Formulary*. Vol. 1. New York and London: Chemical Publishing Co., 1933–1951. Contains formulas for hundreds of liqueurs, but they are rather impractical for use in the home, since most of them are based on essential oils or extracts rather than on natural fruits or herbs. I did find it valuable, however, for getting ideas about good flavor combinations.

Bravery, H. E. *Successful Wine Making at Home*. New York: Gramercy Publishing Co., 1961. Although this book is mainly about wines, it also includes some liqueur recipes. Those for fruit liqueurs produce drinks that are tasty but rather low in alcohol content and more like fortified wine.

Brévans, J. de. *La Fabrication des Liqueurs*. Paris: J. B. Baillére et fils, 1948. An excellent book which treats both large-scale commercial and home manufacture of liqueurs in great detail.

DeKuyper, J. *John DeKuyper's Complete Guide to Cordials*. New York: J. DeKuyper and Sons, 1965. Although this work does not contain any recipes for making cordials, it does give useful descriptions of those that are available, and it also contains good food and drink recipes for cordials.

Distilled Spirits Institute. *1972 Annual Statistical Review*. Washington, D.C.: Distilled Spirits Institute, 1973. The best source of statistics on alcohol beverages sold in the United States.

Fisher, Mary I. *Liqueurs: A Dictionary and Survey*. London: Westminster, 1951. This is an excellent source of historical material on liqueurs, and the author was a descendant of the Wolfschmidt family, which produced a renowned kümmel at Riga, in Latvia.

She managed the London branch of the family business for many years before her death in 1963.

Gibbons, Euell. *Stalking the Healthful Herbs.* New York: David McKay Co., 1966. An excellent field manual on herbs with a good section on wormwood, but the recipe for wormwood cordial was far too strong for my taste.

Grieve, M. *A Modern Herbal.* Vols. 1 and 2. New York: Dover Publications, 1971. This is without doubt the best source of information on herbs that I have found. Literally filled with fascinating information, and it also contains some recipes for fruit brandies and cordials.

Grossman, H. J. *Grossman's Guide to Wines, Spirits, and Beers.* New York: Charles Scribner's Sons, 1964. Has a valuable section on liqueurs and a table of the specific gravity or weight of the various liqueurs, which is helpful if you ever try to make a pousse-café.

Hallgarten, Peter. *Liqueurs.* London: Wine and Spirit Publications, Ltd., 1967. This is the most comprehensive descriptive list of cordials and liqueurs that I have seen. It also contains interesting information about the history of various liqueurs.

Hartmann, G. *Die Frucht Liköre.* C. Knoppe Grüner Verlag und Vertrieb, 1952. The most comprehensive work on fruit cordials and liqueurs that I have seen. There are many recipes for home use, although some are based on extracts.

Henley, Norman W. (ed.). *Henley's 20th Century Formulas.* New York, 1945. Contains several formulas that attempt to simulate Benedictine; however, neither Henley nor anybody else has quite done it. The book nevertheless contains some interesting techniques and procedures.

Hopkins, A. A. (ed.). *Scientific American Cyclopedia of Formulas.* New York: Munn and Co., 1946. Contains many recipes, but they are rather impractical for use in the home, since large quantities and essential oils and chemicals rather than natural products are used. Like Bennett, Hopkins does provide ideas around which recipes can be developed.

Krochmal, A.; Walters, R. S.; Doughty, R. M. *A Guide to Medicinal Plants of Appalachia.* Agricultural Handbook No. 400. Washington, D.C.: U.S. Department of Agriculture, 1971. A good source on medicinal herbs and identification guide if you try to collect your own.

Montagné, Prosper. *Larousse Gastronomique.* New York: Crown Publishers, 1961. A very good source of recipes for liqueurmaking, but requires a lot of conversions, since many quantities are in the metric system.

Schulz, C. G. *Die Liqueur Fabrikation, Theorie und Praxis*. Quedlinburg and Leipzig: Ernst'sche Buchhandlung, 1844. Must have been reprinted, because the copy I found was not that old. This is a very good book with more than 258 recipes.

Trader Vic's Bartender's Guide. Rev. ed. Garden City, N.Y.: Doubleday & Co., 1972. Has a useful glossary of liqueurs and many recipes for mixed drinks using liqueurs.

Index

Abisante, 67
Absinthe, 4, 65
  number 1, 67
  number 2, 68
"Absinthe Drinkers, The" (Toulouse-Lautrec), 66
Alcohol bases, 24–27
Allash kümmel, 49
Allspice, 40
  cordial, 40
Almond
  in allash kümmel, 49
  liqueur, 103
Ananas, crème de, 93
Angelica, 41
  -based liqueurs, 41–44
  number 1, 42
  number 2, 43
  number 3, 43
  number 4, 44
  root, in absinthe number 1, 67
Anise, 44
  -flavored absinthe, 67
  liqueur or anisette, 45
  liqueurs, 44–47
  del Mono, 45
  and orris liqueur, 60
  and rose-hip liqueur, 113
Anise seed in angelica liqueur number 4, 44
Apricot
  jam, in apricot liqueur number 2, 74
  liqueurs, 72–75
    number 1, 73
    number 2, 74
Aquavit, 47, 48

Balm, lemon
  in angelica liqueur number 1, 42
  liqueur, 56
Banana liqueur, 75
Battle of Culloden Moor, 7
Benedictine, 18, 42, 116
Blackberry brandy, *see* Blackberry cordial
Blackberry cordial, 75
Black tea liqueur, 115
Bols, Lucas, 9
The Book of Tea (Okakura), 116
Brandy as alcohol base, 26
Branntwein, 15

Cacao, crème de, 105–107
  number 1, 106
Calvados, 10–11
Canterbury Tales (Chaucer), 10
Caraway
  aquavit, 48
  in celery cordial number 2, 51
  cordial, 48
  Danzig and Goldwasser, 50
  -flavored liqueurs, 47–50
  kümmel, 49
Cassis, crème de, 77
Catherine de Medici, 10, 15
Celery cordials, 50–51
  number 1, 51
  number 2, 51
Cerise, crème de, 78
Charles III of France (the Simple), 10
Chartreuse, 6, 14, 16, 41, 56
  yellow, simulation of, 42
Chaucer, Geoffrey, 10
Cherries jubilee, 20

Index

Cherry Heering, 78, 79
Cherry liqueurs, 78–81
  number 1, 79
  number 2, 80
  number 3, 81
Cherry Suisse, 78
Chocolate liqueurs, 105–107
  crème de cacao number 1, 106
  number 2, 106
Cinnamon and coriander cordial, 52
Citrus fruit liqueurs, 87–91
  grapefruit liqueur number 1, 89
  grapefruit liqueur number 2, 90
  lemon
    cordial, 87
    -lime liqueur, 89
  parfait amour, 88
  three-fruit citrus liqueur, 91
  see also Orange liqueurs
Clarifying agents, 32–34
Clover blossoms, see Red clover
Coffee liqueur, 107
Cointreau, 83
Coloring agents, 29–30
Coltea-blend herb liqueur, 70
Coriander and cinnamon cordial, 52
Crème de ananas, 93
Crème de cacao, 105–107
  number 1, 106
  chocolate liqueur number 2, 106
Crème de cassis, 77
Crème de celery, 50
Crème de cerise, 78
Crème de framboises, 97
Crème de menthe, 17, 57, 58, 118
Crème de recco, 114
Crème de thé, 114
Culloden Moor, Battle of, 7
Culpepper, Nicholas, 45
Curaçao, 83
Currant cordial, 77

Damiana liqueur, 52
Danzig, 47, 50
Danzigwasser, 47
Date cordial, 81
Desserts prepared with liqueurs, 18–20
Distilled Spirits Institutes, 12
D.O.M., 6

Drambuie, 7, 12, 17, 27, 41
  simulation of, 43

Eau de vie, 10, 14, 97
  from plums, 94
Ehrlenmeyer flasks, 22
Eis Liköre, 15
Estrées, Marechal d', 6
Extracts
  commercial sources for, 117
  liqueurs from, 116–118

Fennel, 44
  in absinthe number 1, 67
  in celery cordial number 2, 51
  in kümmel, 49
  liqueurs, 44–47
Filter paper, 22
Flavoring agents, 30
Flower-petal liqueurs, 108–114
  lavender liqueur, 110
  orange-blossom liqueur, 111
  red-clover-blossom liqueur, 112
Forbidden Fruit, 83
  liqueur similar to, 90
Fraise, 99–101
  number 1, 100
  number 2, 100
Framboise, 14, 97
Francis I of France, 5
Fruit, liqueurs with, 19–20, 71–102

Galliano, 41
  simulation of, 43
Geist, 15
Gibbons, Euell, 37, 69
Gin as alcohol base, 27
Ginger cordials, 53–54
  number 1, 54
  number 2, 54
Glen Mist, 8
Glycerine, 24, 29
Goldwasser, 10, 47, 50
Grand Marnier, 15, 83
  simulation of, 85
Grapefruit
  liqueur
    number 1, 89
    number 2, 90

Index

Grapefruit (*cont'd*)
  in three-fruit citrus liqueur, 91
Green tea liqueur, Japanese, 115
Grieve, Mrs. M., 52, 56, 98
Grossman, H. J., 3, 8, 18
Guide to Medicinal Plants of Appalachia (Krochmal et al.), 37
Guide to Wines, Spirits, and Beers (Grossman), 3, 8, 18

Hallgarten, Peter, 6, 8
Hawaiian punch liqueur, 82
Hemingway, Ernest, 5
Henley, Norman W., 34
Henley's 20th Century Formulas, 34
Henry II of France, 10
Herb(s)
  commercial sources for, 38, 45, 56, 70
  liqueurs, history of, 36
  use in liqueur-making, 36
Herbsaint, 67
Honey as sweetening agent, 28

Irish Mist, 7, 27

Japanese green tea liqueur, 115
Jersey Lightning, 2
Juniper berry cordial, 55

Kahlúa, 12, 108
  substitute for, 107
Kennel, Sir Edward, 3
Kir, 78
Kirsch(wasser), 14, 15, 78
Kristal Liköre, 15
Krochmal, Arnold, 37
Kümmel, 9, 47, 49

Labeling, 34
Larousse Gastronomique, 74
Lavender
  liqueur, 110
  petals, commercial source for, 110
Lemon
  cordial, 87
  flavoring in parfait amour, 88
  -lime liqueur, 89

Lemon (*cont'd*)
  in rock and rye, 101
  in three-fruit citrus liqueur, 91
Lemon balm
  in angelica liqueur number 1, 42
  liqueur, 56
Lemon verbena cordial, 65
Licorice, 44
  liqueur or raki, 46
  liqueurs, 44–47
Lime-lemon liqueur, 89
Liqueurs (Hallgarten), 6, 8
Louis XIV of France, 15
Lovage liqueur, 55

MacKinnon family, 7
Manbec, Brother, 6
Maraschino, 78
Mead, 1
Melissa
  in angelica liqueur number 1, 42
  liqueur, 56
Menthe, crème de, 17, 57, 58, 118
Mentzendorff family, 9
Mint
  crème de menthe, 58
  liqueurs and cordials, 57–59
  peppermint cordial, 58
  spearmint cordial, 59
Mirabelle, 14
Modern Herbal, A (Grieve), 98

O Cha, 13
Ojen, 67
Okakura, Kakuzo, 116
Orange(s)
  flavoring in parfait amour, 88
  in grapefruit liqueur number 2, 90
  liqueurs, 83–87
    number 1, 84
    number 2, 85
    number 3, 86
  in rock and rye, 101
  in three-fruit citrus liqueur, 91
Orange blossom(s), 110
  liqueur, 111
Orris root liqueurs, 59–61
  orris root and anise liqueur, 60
  orris root liqueur, 60

Index

Pa-chao, 45
Pahlen, Count, 9
Parfait amour, 88
Peach liqueur, 91
Pear
  cordial, 92
  eaux de vie, 92
Peppermint
  in absinthe number 2, 68
  cordial, 58
Pernod, 67
Peter the Great of Russia, 9
Pineapple liqueur, 93
Plum cordial, 94
Pousse-café, 18
Prune cordial, 95

Quince liqueur, 96

Raspberry cordial, 97
Ratafia, 14
Recco, crème de, 114
Red clover, 111
  -blossom liqueur, 112
Rock and rye, 101
Rose hip(s), 112
  and anise liqueur, 113
Rosemary cordials, 61–62
  number 1, 61
  number 2, 62
Rosalio, 10
Rum as alcohol base, 27
Rumona, 63

Sabra, 83
Serving liqueurs and cordials, 17
Sloe gin, 8
Southern Comfort, 91
Spearmint cordial, 59
Specific gravity, 18

Stalking the Healthful Herbs
  (Gibbons), 37, 69
Star anise, 44
  liqueur, 46
Strawberry cordials, 99–101
  number 1, 100
  number 2, 100
Strega, 4, 41
  simulation of, 44
Stuart, Prince Charles Edward, 7
Sweetening agents, 27

Tea-flavored liqueurs, 114–116
  black tea liqueur, 115
  Japanese green tea liqueur, 115
Thé, crème de, 114
Tia Maria, 107, 108
Tonka bean liqueurs, 63–64
  number 1, 63
  number 2, 64
Toulouse-Lautrec, Henri de, 66
Triple Sec, 83
Tropical fruit–flavored liqueur, 82
"Trou Normand," 11

Van der Hum, 83, 87
Vandermint, 105
Vanilla bean cordial, 64
Verbena cordial, 65
Vincelli, Dom Bernardo, 5
Vodka as alcohol base, 25

Whiskey as alcohol base, 27
Wolfschmidt family, 9
Wormwood, 37, 40, 65
  cordial and absinthe, 65–69
    absinthe number 1, 67
    absinthe number 2, 68
    wormwood cordial, 69

Zebrovka, 69